Critical Guides to French T

20 Racine: Phèdre

Critical Guides to French Texts

EDITED BY ROGER LITTLE, WOLFGANG VAN EMDEN, DAVID WILLIAMS

RACINE

Phèdre

Second edition

J.P. Short

Formerly Senior Lecturer in French
University of Sheffield

Grant & Cutler Ltd
1998

© Grant & Cutler Ltd 1998
ISBN 0 7293 0408 6

First edition 1983
Second edition 1998

DEPÓSITO LEGAL: V. 4.022 - 1998

Printed in Spain by Artes Gráficas Soler, S.A., Valencia for
GRANT & CUTLER LTD
55-57 GREAT MARLBOROUGH STREET, LONDON W1V 2AY

Contents

Foreword

It is indeed remarkable to note the amount of attention that Racine and seventeenth-century literature as a whole have received since this study of *Phèdre* was first published. Although it has not been rewritten for this reprint the bibliography has been updated to take account of the new work that has been done. The titles listed are those of works which explore original and fruitful ways of understanding Racine both in the study and, especially, on the stage. The role of speech and language, for instance, has been brought to the fore in ways not examined so fully previously. These approaches have not provoked the uproar which greeted the *nouvelle critique* in the sixties when it was applied to the tragedies of Racine. The uproar has died down but the influence of the *nouvelle critique* has by no means disappeared and has added to the variety and diversity of Racinian criticism which has so much renewed the study of his tragedies. It would be wrong, of course, to concentrate entirely on new works and neglect those which paved the way for much that came later and have never been superseded. My own approach which is traditional in some ways nevertheless shows, I hope, awareness of trends which were to be developed and examined subsequently. My aim is to stimulate debate and as the last word on *Phèdre* will never be said there is some virtue, perhaps, in keeping the discussion going.

Prefatory Note

There are many modern editions of *Phèdre*, either by itself or in editions of the complete works of Racine. Some of these are listed in the bibliography. I have used the one, easily available, edited by Philippe Drouillard and Denis A. Canal, published by Larousse in the Classiques Larousse series, and all line references are to that. Italicised numbers in parentheses, followed by page references, refer to numbered items in the bibliography at the end of this volume.

Introduction

Phèdre is one of the summits of French literature. To attempt to
scale it is a hazardous undertaking. To do so within the confines
of the present study may seem foolhardy to many. Yet the attempt is worth making. The very fact that it is impossible to take
into account everything that has been written on the subject of
Racine's masterpiece makes necessary a concentration which, it
is hoped, will at least yield up the essence of the tragedy. This is
the justification for my approach. I am above all concerned that
the reader is made aware of the differing elements that have
gone into the making of the play which, in turn, impart to it its
uniqueness. To do this we must distinguish between those
elements which are the common coin of seventeenth-century
French tragedy and those which are the contribution of Racine.
This is to over-simplify somewhat, because Racine's contribution consists in the way that he uses elements common to all
writers of tragedy in the period, but in a way peculiar to himself.
The tragedy that Racine wrote could not have been written had
the form, developed during the seventeenth century in France,
not existed. It was because of this form that a new kind of
tragedy was discovered or rather, to be more precise, a new way
of looking at the tragic implications of human existence was
evolved. *Phèdre* is one of the most striking examples of this.
Using a theme which had been treated on numerous previous occasions Racine makes an original tragic statement. The aim of
the study that follows is to try to show in what that originality
consists while, at the same time, suggesting ways of interpreting
the text which will bring out not only the tragic meaning of
Phèdre but also its dramatic force. *Phèdre* is a play, and the
casting of the story of the daughter of Minos and Pasiphaé into
a dramatic mould, and a very specific dramatic mould at that,
must be acknowledged as one of the elements which it is fruitful
to explore. Ideas, emotions, reactions are expressed in speeches,

in conversations between the people involved. Racine's methods of bringing these situations, these conversations into existence are clearly an important factor in any attempt to explain and appreciate the meaning of the play. These are the considerations which are behind the discussion of *Phèdre* which is offered here.

The text of *Phèdre* presents no problems. The version which is now almost always printed is that which is found in the complete edition of his works which Racine published in 1697, the last before his death in 1699. The first edition appeared in March 1677 shortly after the first run of the play in January of that year. There are no significant variations between the texts of 1677 and 1697 except, perhaps, for one which is worth mentioning. When the play was first published it was called *Phèdre et Hippolyte*. It was only in the edition published in 1687 that it became *Phèdre* and Racine maintained that title in 1697 and so it has remained ever since. If this has any significance it is to be found, possibly, in the fact that this was the first time that Racine had used two names in the title of one of his plays. Hitherto one had sufficed: *Andromaque*, *Britannicus*, *Bérénice* etc. By putting some emphasis on Hippolyte in this way, even if he removed it later on, Racine gives a clue to an aspect of his tragedy which should not be ignored. The role of Hippolyte, often said to be overshadowed by that of Phèdre, must be given the attention that it deserves if the tragedy is to be fully understood.

1. Some Aspects of Form

When Racine started to write *Phèdre*, possibly about two years before its first performance on 1 January 1677, he was the author of nine plays, eight tragedies and one comedy, which had been written at fairly regular intervals between 1664 and 1674. When he began his career as a dramatist the form of tragedy which he was to use was more or less fixed. The process by which it had evolved to become what it was in the 1660s in France had been long and complicated and there is no need to trace the story.[1] What is relevant is the effect that the form of tragedy had on the way a dramatist treated a subject which he had chosen for his play. There can be no doubt that the form of seventeenth-century French tragedy had a profound effect on the whole concept of tragedy as such. That is to say that the fact that the dramatist was obliged to turn his material into a dramatic form changed the tragic meaning of that material. By the time that Racine came to write *Phèdre* he had perfected his technique and was a master of it. As the material which he used was readily available in the many plays that had already been written on this theme, the way that he used it can be explored in order to find the meaning he gave to it, which is what this study will attempt to do. It will be an exploration of *Phèdre* which will consider how Racine dealt dramatically with the subject he chose, what effects he sought and the means used to achieve them, thus reaching, it is hoped, an understanding of its tragic meaning.

When the plays that Racine had written before *Phèdre* are considered a pattern does emerge. All deal with a small group of people (the theatrical conditions of the seventeenth century precluded the writing of plays which demanded large casts) closely linked by ties either of relationship (father/son or daughter, mother/son or daughter) or love which can be either

---

[1] The history of tragedy in France in the seventeenth century has been extensively treated. See Adam (*9*), Bray (*11*), Brereton (*12*), Lanson (*14*).

mutual or unrequited. The nature and implications of these links are then examined by placing the group into a situation which demands action and reaction dictated by the preocupations of the members of the group and which will reveal to them, if they were unaware of it before, that their aspirations of love or power are doomed and that there is no hope that they will ever be realised. The conditions that bring about these consequences vary and can seem to spring from inexplicable causes or from the nature of the people themselves. When it is a question of unrequited love there is no difficulty of interpretation, as this love can be shown to be the cause of the tragedy. Where, however, external forces are at work the case becomes more complicated and less easy to understand, and it is precisely in this area that the arguments about the meaning of Racinian tragedy are most acute.

The opinion that Racine's view of the world and hence his conception of tragedy was very much influenced by his upbringing among Jansenists is not now held as widely as it once was.[2] It has been pointed out that the kind of situations which Racine describes were to be found in other seventeenth-century works and that the picture of humanity which emerges from his tragedies is not exclusive to him. Indeed it hardly needs instruction in Jansenist thinking to come to the conclusion that men bear within themselves the seeds of their own destruction and that unrestrained attempts to assuage violent passions are very dangerous. Therefore in considering the nature of the tragic world that Racine constructs for us it could be said that it is scarcely necessary to look much further than the ordinary knowledge of human nature available to every thinking and observant man of whatever age he happens to live in. What we need to look for in Racine is an understanding of the way he succeeded in conveying these truths about human nature so effectively that his plays continue to fascinate and enthral. What did Racine have at his disposal in order to do this? A knowledge, very deep and detailed, of the literature of Greece and Rome; a dramatic form unlike any other that had existed before; and his

---

[2]An interesting discussion of Racine and Jansenism can be found in Sellier (*41*).

own experience of life. We know quite a lot about the first two of these and speculate, not always very successfully, about the third. One of the virtues of modern criticism of Racine, however, is that it has suggested ways of thinking about the tragedies which take this aspect into account and which are fruitful. Previous attempts to relate Racine's life to his works have only succeeded in making suggestions which add very little to the appreciation of his tragedies.[3]

Racine had a profound knowledge of the works of the three great Greek writers of tragedies, Aeschylus, Sophocles and Euripides. His annotations of the works of these dramatists show the detailed study he had made of them. The study of these, in their turn, is a method of speculating about Racine's own ideas on tragic themes and the creation of emotion by dramatic means. These tragedies deal with a limited number of subjects. The Trojan war with its consequences for the families of Priam and Agamemnon is one; the story of Œdipus and his family is another. They show the violence of which passion is capable, be it love, hatred, ambition or revenge. In four of his tragedies Racine used material which came from these plays, amongst other sources. They are *La Thébaïde* (1664), *Andromaque* (1667), *Iphigénie* (1674) and *Phèdre* (1667), and the changes he made in his treatment of the subjects and the significance of those changes insofar as *Phèdre* is concerned will be discussed below. It is hardly necessary to say that Racine chose those aspects of the legends which allowed him to develop his own concept of tragedy. It is worth noting at this point that war is an important element in all these stories save that of *Phèdre* itself, although even in this play Thésée is a warrior and Hippolyte is ready to go to war to uphold his rights to the throne of Athens. The relevance of this concerns the heroic status of the characters and the values which they uphold. It is against a background of such values that the interplay of passion has to be seen, and the full meaning of Racine's conception of tragedy will not be appreciated if this is not taken into account. The nature

---

[3] The most controversial of these is the attempt made by René Jasinski in *Vers le vrai Racine* (Paris: Armand Colin, 1958) to relate not only Racine's life but many contemporary events to the subject-matter of the tragedies.

of the obstacles which prevent passions taking an unhindered course in their attempt to be satisfied have often to do with an ideal based on heroic behaviour which manifests itself in war. Assumptions about what constitutes admissible behaviour are inherent in the judgements which characters in these tragedies make, either on themselves or on others. It sometimes seems to be forgotten that Racine assumes very similar standards of value, as distinct from behaviour, on the part of his characters, to those of Corneille. The point is worth bearing in mind when Racine's concept of tragedy is being considered. Of Racine's five other secular tragedies, three, *Britannicus* (1669), *Bérénice* (1670) and *Mithridate* (1673) have their source in Roman history; one, *Alexandre* (1665) in Greek history and one, *Bajazet* (1672) in modern Turkish history. This last play provides us with an interesting clue to one aspect of Racine's conception of tragedy. Justifying his choice of a subject taken from modern history he says that 'l'éloignement des pays répare en quelque sorte la trop grande proximité des temps' for 'les personnages tragiques doivent être regardés d'un autre œil que nous ne regardons d'ordinaire les personnages que nous avons vus de si près' (Preface to *Bajazet*). Distance thus confers on the Turks the tragic dignity which is essential and which time bestows on the Greeks and Romans of the other tragedies. This is interesting because it suggests to us that, in watching a tragedy by Racine we are watching people who are, in some degree, removed from ourselves and not like us. How can they, then, be representative? This is where the art of Racine comes into the question, and in trying to find the answer we must attempt to understand what causes the effect his characters undoubtedly have. By choosing subjects which are remote in time and space Racine is deliberately seeking to invest his tragic characters with an aura of being different from ordinary human beings. It is this aura which will contribute, in a way that I hope to demonstrate, to the tragic meaning of these characters which will, paradoxically, relate them very closely to ordinary human beings.

The subjects that Racine chose to treat had to be adapted to the dramatic form that he was going to use. This form was fixed, as has been said, and there is no evidence that Racine ever thought of innovating or changing the form that he found in existence when he started writing his tragedies. In order to understand the problems which were presented by the use of this form it is necessary to discuss some aspects of it, particularly the influence of the three unities and the notions of *vraisemblance* and *bienséance*.

The rule of the three unities had been elaborated in the course of the sixteenth and seventeenth centuries from indications in the *Poetics* of Aristotle who, however, made no mention of the unity of place. The three unities were those of time, place and action and were intended to be used so that the dramatic action should unfold itself in a short space of time in a given place. The duration of the time and the extent of the space were matters never completely agreed and there was much discussion of their meaning when the first attempts were made in the 1630s to apply them. The quarrel which followed the first performance of Corneille's play *Le Cid* in 1637, a play in which the unities were supposed to have been observed, helped to give some definition to the meaning of these terms and by the time that Racine began to write, it was generally accepted that the unity of time was to be roughly a day and by day was meant the hours of daylight. The action of a play would begin in the morning, possibly the early morning (as Racine makes clear, for instance, in *Britannicus* and *Iphigénie*), continue through the day and draw to its close in the late afternoon or evening. Much has been written on the skill with which Racine introduces past time into his tragedies, and it has been shown how effectively he uses the past to create a background to the action which allows him to range far beyond the confines of the mere few hours which the events in the play actually need for their accomplishment. This method of transcending the limitations placed on him by the need to observe the unity of time is thus turned into a powerful asset which immeasurably widens and deepens the action. The place in which the action occurred could be a whole town, though generally this was not the case in the time of Racine, or a palace or a single room in a palace. The need to observe this unity taxed the ingenuity of playwrights to the utmost and Racine was one of the few who were able to construct a dramatic action which could be supposed to take place in a single room without stretching credibility to unacceptable lengths.

While it is not difficult to describe what is meant by the unities of time and place, the same is not true of the unity of action. It would not be unfair to say that there was no agreement in the seventeenth century on this matter. Corneille's interpretation was very different from Racine's, although this assumes that it is possible to know what Racine's interpretation was and this would be a very rash assertion to make. Who can say in what the action of a play consists? The mere recounting of the plot does not really illuminate what actually happens on the stage and the relationship between what happens on the stage and the plot of the play is often surprising. We shall have occasion to talk of this with reference to *Phèdre* in trying to establish what the tragedy is about. However, there are certain things that can be said about the unity of action which do help in understanding some of the effects which it had on the way a play was put together. It should not be possible to take anything away from the play, any character, any scene, any episode, without destroying the meaning and sense of the whole. Everything that goes into the making of the play should be pointing in one direction, and that direction is what is called the action. Or again, the action of the play can be considered as being the same as the subject of a picture. Everything in the picture contributes in some degree to the interpretation and comprehension of the picture and the picture is assumed to be a representation of something that can be defined. Similarly in a play everything can be thought to contribute to the presentation of a single theme which constitutes the action. None of this is, however, very satisfactory and does not shed a great deal of light on the meaning of the unity of action. This need not upset us overmuch as what we can do is try to understand the effect on a play of the desire to observe the unity of action. What we see is concentration and an attempt to eliminate certain kinds of extraneous matter from the treatment of a subject. By certain kinds I mean sub-plots, the undue development of pointers in the story which would lead away from the direction in which the plot seems to be moving, and the introduction of characters who have nothing to do with the matter in hand. All this certainly had an effect on the way a dramatist approached his subject, and it will be as well to bear this in mind when considering Racine's treatment of the subject of *Phèdre*.

The first thing to be noticed is that in order to observe the unities the dramatist was obliged to make a choice from the material he was using for his play. Whether he was leafing through the historians of Greece and Rome or the tragedies of Aeschylus, Sophocles, Euripides or Seneca he would, of necessity, have to eliminate an enormous amount of detail and decide on what aspect of a life or on what episode in a life he was going to concentrate. There would be no question of his trying to recount the whole of anybody's life or even a substantial part of it. He needed to be able to seize on one moment, one day in a life which by some means or other could be made to express the meaning of the whole of that life. As far as Racine is concerned it is easy to point out, on a superficial level, how he coped with the problem. He chooses a day on which something happens which releases violent forces which have hitherto been kept under control. He thus assumes a long period of time, before the action of the play starts, during which those forces have had time to come into being and to develop.

This raises the question of the part the past plays and how it is introduced and the interplay of past and present in the action of the play. How Racine chooses the day and how he prepares for it will be discussed with reference to *Phèdre* below, but here I ought perhaps to explain what I mean by stating that it is easy on a superficial level to say what Racine does. I mean that Racine's use of time and place is very subtle, as has often been pointed out, and to assume that one has explained the technique of Racine by drawing attention to his clever manipulation of these aspects of the drama is to reveal oneself unaware of the more important sides of this question. Racine's use of time and space should be regarded as clues which indicate to us a way of looking at his conception of tragedy which can be very revealing. For instance, the need for something to be accomplished in the course of one day forces the pace of events and precipitates the people concerned into actions and decisions with very great consequences.

Thus in Racine's tragedies characters are frequently called upon to make irreversible decisions in a very short space of time, decisions which are going to have terrible effects on their existence. One thinks of Andromaque, of Junie, of Bajazet and of course of Phèdre (the accusation of Hippolyte) and it becomes clear that Racine is here using the necessity of observing the unity of time to shape his interpretation of tragedy. Other consequences are perhaps too obvious to need underlining: the necessity of relating the events which happen in the course of the play to a time span no greater than twelve hours or thereabouts; the impossibility of allowing the characters much freedom of movement (unless they leave the play altogether they must not stray far from the place where the action is supposed to be happening); the need to overcome a sense of fixity so that the characters do not appear frozen in a moment of time. The impression must be given of a life being lived even though only one day of that life is on show. These are all points which the dramatist has to bear in mind and which, inevitably, affect his presentation of his subject.

The problems posed by the unity of place are as great, if not greater than those posed by the unity of time. It is not hard to imagine the difficulty of deciding on a spot where it is probable that a number of different people with different interests and different relationships with each other should be able to meet. Since we are nearly always dealing with situations involving two sides of a question with two opposing sets of people it is clear that it is not going to be easy to imagine a place where it is probable that each side may meet separately and meet together. The difficulty is so great that some dramatists could not solve it and fell back on the device of using two rooms in the same building. Another solution was to be vague and never specify exactly where the events are occurring. Racine's method of dealing with this problem drew near to this without actually reaching it. He is not unspecific in the places where he sets his tragedies but neither is he too specific. *Andromaque* takes place in 'une salle du palais de Pyrrhus'; *Bérénice* (very precisely) 'dans un cabinet qui est entre l'appartement de Titus et celui de Bérénice'.

Mithridate, on the other hand, is very vague: 'la scène est à Nymphée, port de mer sur le Bosphore Cimmérien, dans le Taurique Chersonèse'. Here there is no mention of a palace, let alone a room in one. *Iphigénie* returns to a stated place: 'la scène est en Aulide, dans la tente d'Agamemnon'. Finally, our own play, *Phèdre*, resembles *Mithridate* in lack of definiteness: 'la scène est à Trézène, ville du Péloponnèse'. The significance, if any, of the setting of *Phèdre* will be discussed below. Here I am more concerned with the restraints placed on the dramatist by the unity of place and its effect on the play.

It is clear that by reducing the field of action to one or even two particular spots, the range of events which can be shown on the stage becomes very limited. Life does not arrange itself neatly in this way, and events which may have a profound influence on an individual may happen a long way away from where he is. Or again, an individual may embark on a course of action which will take him far from his starting point. All of this kind of activity is ruled out for the dramatist observing the unity of place. What cannot be shown must be related. This simple and obvious fact had a profound effect not only on the dramatic disposition of a subject but also on the very interpretation of tragedy itself. For the whole focus of interest was altered and events came to be considered of secondary importance (as they could not be shown) and the effect of events on people became the centre of attention. This is to oversimplify somewhat but at least it points us in the direction in which we should be looking. In the tragedies of Racine things are going to happen but the interesting things that happen are not always those which one might expect from reading an account of the story which he is dramatising. The fact that this is so springs, to a certain extent, from the need to observe the unities.

A further word on the unity of action is called for. I have indicated above some of the problems connected with the understanding of what is meant by this unity, and it can be acknowledged that the examination of Racine's tragedies does not help to clarify the issue. He talks about action in various of his prefaces but in ways that do not throw much light on those aspects of it we are trying to elucidate. In the prefaces to

Britannicus and *Bérénice* he praises simplicity as being the most desirable ingredient in the action of a tragedy. He gives his approbation to 'une action qui se passe en un seul jour, et qui s'avançant par degrés vers sa fin, n'est soutenue que par les intérêts, les sentiments et les passions des personnages' (Preface to *Britannicus*) and to 'une action simple, soutenue de la violence des passions, de la beauté des sentiments, et de l'élégance de l'expression' (Preface to *Bérénice*). In both these cases Racine is opposing his view to another which would fill the action of the play with a large number of things happening. So action for Racine here seems to mean the events which happen, or which are referred to as happening, in the course of the play. This does not help greatly with the concept of the unity of action, as action, in this sense of things happening, could be simple without being unified. Thus, although the action of *Bérénice* is simple if it is thought of as being the sending away of Bérénice from Rome by Titus, such a description does not correspond at all to what actually happens in the play. If it is difficult to pin down the concept of the unity of action in *Bérénice*, generally considered the least complicated of Racine's tragedies, how much more difficult it is to do in *Phèdre*. Yet the concept is there, and it had an influence. What the influence was insofar as *Phèdre* is concerned will be considered in a later chapter.

I have spent some time on this question of the unities because it seems to me that they can be used as pointers to an approach to Racine's concept of tragedy. It is obvious that his treatment of the subject of *Phèdre* was determined, to some extent, by these rules and therefore the way his imagination was set working can be illuminated, and this will form part of the way that my discussion will develop.

There are the two further notions of *vraisemblance* and *bienséance* (or *bienséances*) which must be mentioned before moving on to the tragedy itself. The concepts that these words represent are easy to grasp, but what is less easy is to reconcile concept with practice, or rather to determine exactly what any author thought he was doing when he was observing *vraisemblance*. This was supposed, for instance, to rule out unvarnished fact as the subject of a play, as often unvarnished fact could strain credibility. Truth can be stranger than fiction. Fiction, however, was ruled out, as imagination, if given a free rein, could go even further in straining credibility. What was required, therefore, was a subject rooted in fact but tempered by a sense of the possible. In other words the imagination was allowed to work in one direction, that of changing facts to accord with the knowledge of what was within the bounds of possibility, but not in another, that of inventing facts.

The distinction may seem hard to grasp when one considers what both Corneille and Racine did with their factual sources. Events were telescoped or stretched out far beyond the dates of their actual happening; people's lives were prolonged or shortened without the slightest compunction, children were born who never had been born and others were killed off without trace; characters were invented where history had unfortunately failed to respond to the needs of a situation. None of this matters, of course, except insofar as it actually allows us to see the playwright's imagination at work, and this is where *vraisemblance* is so useful. It suggests a frame which the playwright has in mind when he sets to work, a frame in which something is going to take shape and which will help to determine that shape. It rules out certain possibilities which the playwright might have considered and suggests others that he uses.

The complexity involved, however, can be illustrated from *Phèdre*. Why does Racine invent the character of Aricie? It would appear from what he himself says in the preface to *Phèdre* that this character was invented to make Hippolyte more *vraisemblable*, that is to say less of a 'philosophe exempt de toute imperfection' and more of a young man with normal instincts. Yet this same Hippolyte is killed by a most *invraisemblable* monster from the sea. It may be objected that this is not to see the question in its true light but I am making the point because it will be an aim of this study to show that there is no great incompatibility or inconsistency here. On the contrary the awareness of this kind of thinking on *vraisemblance* can be most useful in considering the distinction between what matters in a tragedy of Racine and what is only of secondary importance.

As for *bienséance*, the word has two aspects. One dealt with the propriety of certain actions and words and was a consequence of the desire, earlier in the seventeenth century, to rid the stage of obscene or violent events and language. It resulted in the somewhat limited vocabulary (though not as limited as used to be thought, as studies of Racine's vocabulary show) which could be used in the expression of ideas and in the description of events, and in the reduction of physical action on the stage to a minimum. Once more this is a challenge, and the way in which Racine meets that challenge when dealing with a subject full of violence and sexual passion such as *Phèdre* is a measure of his art which it behoves us to appreciate. The other aspect of *bienséance* is concerned with the need not to contradict too blatantly accepted ideas of behaviour and comportment. Boileau put it like this:

> Qu'Agamemnon soit fier, superbe, intéressé;
> Que pour ses dieux Enée ait un respect austère.
> Conservez à chacun son propre caractère.
> Des siècles, des pays étudiez les mœurs:
> Les climats font souvent les diverses humeurs.[4]

How far this was what playwrights actually did is rather open to question, but it is useful to remember that the concept of *bienséance* enabled them to build their presentation of a subject on a foundation of accepted ideas. There was much that did not have to be explained because it could be assumed that the audience would be thinking along certain lines. Racine uses this notion, for instance, in his treatment of power and those who wield it, and in his treatment of young love. There is available a stereotype which can be copied but, and this must not be forgotten, the stereotype never takes over the role. It is only used as a base on which to build and as such it has its place. Because we know what that base is we can draw some conclusions about the nature of the originality which appears in the finished product.

Let me try to summarise, as far as Racine is concerned, what has been said so far. Racine looks to Greek or Roman history or mythology (mythology was considered the equivalent of history

[4] Boileau, *Art poétique*, Chant III, 110-14.

for this purpose) for the subjects of his plays. He chooses aspects of this subject which can be brought together in accordance with the exigencies of the unities of time and place, including something here, rejecting something there and, if necessary for his purpose, inventing. An action is brought into being, using the word action here in the sense of a series of events following one upon the other which are given a place in space and time, a very narrow place as has been indicated, and which conform, more or less, to certain fairly clear-cut criteria of what is possible in human behaviour (if not what is probable), and which reach a conclusion which may be death for some of the people involved but which, at all events, will mean a very sharp cleavage between the present, that is the events of the play, and any future that the characters could be supposed to have. In other words, the action of the play will represent a moment of existence which will have never-ending repercussions for those involved.

2. Some Aspects of Subject

Racine was far from the first dramatist to treat the subject of Phaedra and her love for her stepson Hippolytus.[5] Euripides had written two tragedies on the subject, of which only one survives, and Seneca had followed Euripides, probably using as his model the tragedy that has not survived. In France Robert Garnier wrote *Hippolyte*, published in 1573, while in the seventeenth century no less than four dramatists turned their hand to the subject: La Pinelière in 1635, Gilbert in 1646, Bidar in 1675 and Pradon in the same year as Racine, 1677, and in direct competition with him.[6] As well as these treatments of the subject there were several plays which dealt with the love of a stepmother for her stepson. The history of this theme has been well catalogued and it is not my purpose to write another such history. What is to the point is to show that, in choosing the subject of *Phèdre*, Racine was choosing a subject that was well known and one with which his audience could be expected to be familiar. Georges May drew attention to this aspect of Racine's method and came to the conclusion that it showed that what Racine wanted when treating a subject dramatically was not to depend for the interest of the audience on the shock of novelty, the desire to know what happens next, but to arouse the interest in the way he dealt with a subject, the outcome of which was well known in advance. This is a helpful suggestion, but is not the whole story as H.T. Barnwell has shown.[7]

[5] The history of the theme of Phèdre and Hippolyte in French literature has been fully treated by Newton (*36*) and Francis (*23*). To these should be added the discussion devoted by Jean Pommier to the same theme in (*40*).

[6] I do not propose to go into the question of the Pradon-Racine confrontation over putting on plays on the same subject at the same time. There are full accounts of this episode of literary history in Adam (*9*) and Picard (*38*).

[7] See Barnwell (*19*) passim.

Racine did not disdain the use of surprise and the unexpected and although he never, as Corneille did frequently, brought his action to what seemed a happy ending only to send it off in another direction at the beginning of the following act, he often left a situation in suspense at the end of one act with the spectator wondering what will happen, the answer being given at the beginning of the following act (cf. *Andromaque*, Act III, sc.viii and Act IV, sc.i). The conclusion of Georges May needs to be modified then. He can be followed, I think, in as much as Racine was not particularly concerned with springing a surprise on his audience by the dénouement of his tragedies, but it is not right to suggest that he was uninterested in the effects of surprise within the tragedy itself. Thus his treatment of a subject still very much depends on his interpretation of it, and this interpretation can best be penetrated by considering the changes he makes to his original material and the way in which he conducts the action.

By choosing well-known subjects he has the advantage of being able to avail himself to the utmost of the associations which the subject brings in its wake. He would not be able to do this by choosing obscure corners of history or mythology to dramatise. Thus in *Phèdre* he will exploit to the full the evocative force of the legend, and the legendary figures who are part of it, and this becomes a very important element in the construction of the tragedy. In any consideration of the subject of *Phèdre* then, two things must be borne in mind. One is the fact that the broad outlines of the story, as recounted in the various sources which Racine used, will be followed. The other is that, within this framework, Racine will feel free to invent for himself the way the action unfolds and the kind of scenes that he will write to convey the meaning of the tragedy. Bearing this in mind, it is time to turn to the subject which Racine decided to treat sometime after 1674, the year of *Iphigénie*.

In choosing the latter subject Racine said that he had always wanted to treat it, but had hesitated to do so because he could not bring himself to write a play in which he would have to 'souiller la scène par le meurtre horrible d'une personne aussi vertueuse et aussi aimable qu'il fallait représenter Iphigénie'

(Preface to *Iphigénie*). Either Racine believed in a universe in which the good are spared and the evil punished, in other words a universe ruled by justice and properly expressed in melodrama, or he considered that the meaningless killing of an innocent victim was not tragic. In this Racine would simply be following Aristotle who had written that to present a good man passing from happiness to misery was a form of plot to be avoided. Such a situation, he said, is neither fear-inspiring nor piteous, but simply 'odious'.[8] The point is of importance as far as the choice of the story of Phèdre and Hippolyte is concerned because it immediately suggests a way of looking at both one and the other. The theme of justice is one which runs through *Phèdre*, and the death of Hippolyte poses a problem from this point of view. At the moment when it seems that Iphigénie is going to be killed it turns out that the real victim is Eriphile, another Iphigénie whose identity is revealed only at that moment, and who is a much more appropriate victim than Agamemnon's daughter if it is accepted that only those who commit evil deeds deserve to be punished. At the moment of Hippolyte's death, though, no substitute appears to take his place in spite of the fact that he is as guiltless as Iphigénie. Nothing could be more unjust than the death of Hippolyte. But is there justice in what happens to Phèdre?

The answer to both these questions tells us something about the reasons Racine treated the subject in the way that he did. For the invention of Aricie has something, though not everything, to do with a wish to make Hippolyte less 'innocent', and thus introduce what might seem to be a semblance of justice into his fate. As for Phèdre, it is at once apparent that there is a very big difference between her and the heroines of the tragedies that had gone before. As portrayed by Euripides, Phèdre condemns herself for the love she feels and this is the element that Racine takes and develops. Before creating Phèdre, Racine had painted three women who were victims of a violent, sensual and unrequited love: Hermione, Roxane and Eriphile. None of these had felt any sense of guilt, and all were prepared to act immorally in

8 Aristotle, *On the Art of Poetry*, translated by Ingram Bywater (Oxford: Clarendon Press, 1954), p.50.

pursuit of the satisfaction of their passion. Now Phèdre resembles these in the nature of her passion, but because of her moral outlook she has affinities with the other line of Racinian heroines who pursue the path of virtue: Andromaque, Junie, Bérénice, Atalide, Monime and Iphigénie. It is precisely this which makes the originality of Phèdre and gives Racine the opportunity of exploring in this tragedy a situation which he had not attempted before.

Let us consider for a moment the nature of the subject as found in the *Hippolytus* of Euripides. I do not propose to go into this in any great detail, but it is worth bearing in mind some of the main lines of the subject as treated by the Greek dramatist. The important thing to remember is that Euripides sees the subject as a conflict between the goddesses Aphrodite, the goddess of love, and Artemis, the goddess of hunting. Hippolytus refuses to worship at the altar of Aphrodite who takes her revenge on him by causing his stepmother, Phaedra, to fall in love with him and be, consequently, responsible for making a false accusation against him, when he refuses her love. This will result in his death. Phaedra is depicted as a woman dominated by a passion which she abhors, but she kills herself half way through the tragedy and the main interest is concentrated on Hippolytus, sent to his death by Theseus, who is deceived by the note accusing Hippolytus which Phaedra leaves behind her when she hangs herself. These are the broad outlines of the story which Racine found in Euripides. Seneca's play differed from that of Euripides in that his Phaedra is much less conscious of wrong-doing and, indeed, makes a determined effort to seduce Hippolytus.

I do not propose to take these accounts further. I am concerned simply to draw attention to some salient points in the ancient plays, and use these as a basis for the discussion of Racine's play. The question which presents itself right at the beginning is that of the relationship between man and the gods, and as this is relevant to the interpretation of *Phèdre* it must be considered. It was not at all wonderful, to the Greek audience, that gods should seem to possess the characteristics of men; that they should be vengeful, passionate, jealous, possessive. They

are, in fact, a reflection on an enlarged scale of human beings
and their weaknesses. That men should be the victims of such
forces seemed, and still seems, natural. It is a convenient ex-
planation of the passions that drive men to violent action, and it
is also convenient for the dramatist to have at his disposal a way
of looking at human affairs which makes a very effective
dramatic system. Now is this what Racine does in *Phèdre*? Does
he take over completely the framework suggested by Euripides
and transfer it, with suitable changes, to his play? Is he showing
a world in which the gods use human beings as their playthings,
a world in which there is not very much freedom for men to
guide their own destinies as they will? In my opinion this is not
the case. It is noteworthy that in his tragedies Racine avoids the
use of the supernatural where he can. The case of *Iphigénie* ob-
viously springs to mind. Racine says quite categorically 'quelle
apparence encore de dénouer ma tragédie par le secours d'une
déesse et d'une machine, et par une métamorphose qui pouvait
bien trouver quelque créance du temps d'Euripide, mais qui
serait trop absurde et trop incroyable parmi nous?' (Preface to
Iphigénie).

This is to state clearly that Racine did not believe that it was
possible for gods to intervene directly in the affairs of men. If it
had not been for Eriphile he would not have written *Iphigénie*. Is
it likely then that he would, when treating the subject of *Phèdre*,
have postulated a situation which demanded for its understanding the view that men's actions are the result of supernatural
forces at work? Hardly. Racine banishes Artemis and Aphrodite
from his tragedy. Certainly there are frequent references to
Venus (Racine uses the Roman not the Greek name of this goddess) but Artemis, or Diana, does not appear. There is only one
reference to Diana in the tragedy and that occurs in Act V, scene i
when Hippolyte is promising Aricie to marry her and to seek the
protection of the gods on their union:

> Des dieux les plus sacrés j'attesterai le nom,
> Et la chaste Diane, et l'auguste Junon. (1403-4)

It is Neptune who takes the place of Diana as the god whom

Hippolyte worships and his is the name that recurs frequently. What the role of Venus and Neptune is will be discussed later. At this point it is sufficient to say that here it is proposed to treat *Phèdre* as a play that is concerned with human beings and dealing with human affairs.

Does this help us to understand the subject of *Phèdre*? In order to understand the subject of the tragedy it is not enough simply to recount the plot. Let me explain what I mean. Suppose I were to tell the story of *Phèdre* as follows, would it make it clear what the play is about? Phèdre, wife of Thésée, falls in love with the latter's son Hippolyte by a former wife Antiope. She keeps this love secret for years, but is at last persuaded by her nurse and confidante, Œnone, to reveal it to her. Just after doing this, news is brought that her husband is dead. Going to see Hippolyte to plead with him to look after her children, she cannot refrain from talking to him about herself, and is brought to the point where she confesses to him that she loves him. Before this happens we have already learned that Hippolyte himself is in love with Aricie, a girl who has been forbidden by Thésée ever to marry. Hippolyte is horrified by his stepmother's declaration of love and repulses her. Soon after this it is announced that the news of Thésée's death is false, and that not only is he not dead but he is on the point of arriving in Trézène, where these events are taking place. Terrified of the consequences of what she has done Phèdre allows Œnone to calumniate Hippolyte by telling Thésée that he had tried to seduce her. In a fury Thésée prays to Neptune to avenge him, which the god does by sending a monster out of the sea which frightens the horses drawing Hippolyte's chariot as he drives off into exile, and he is killed. Phèdre commits suicide, but before she dies she reveals the truth to Thésée.

This is one way of saying what the play is about. It would in fact be possible to recount these same events in innumerable different ways and it is an amusing and often revealing exercise to see in how many ways an account, such as that given above, can be written simply by putting the emphasis on different aspects of the story and altering the order in which the events are presented. What this proves, it seems to me, is that giving an ac-

count of this kind does not represent accurately what happens in
the play. These events should only be considered as excuses for
provoking certain situations which provide the means for expressing a tragic interpretation of human existence. In *Phèdre*
this takes the form of examining the conflict that arises in a
human being when the desires of the flesh collide with moral
values. Because this is a play, this examination is in a dramatic
form and thus we have a plot in which characters are given
words to say and things to do. It is the relationship between what
is said and done and the way that it is said and done that constitutes the area in which the real subject of the play should be
sought. In *Phèdre*, as in other Racinian tragedies, form, which
has already been discussed, is of great importance in this connec-
tion. There is also the question of the part played by the supernatural. If we put on one side the view that the goddesses Venus
and Diana are not directly involved because the play is not about
the conflict between them, as in Euripides, we are still left with
the awkward question of Neptune. Thésée prays to Neptune to
avenge him on Hippolyte, and Neptune responds by sending a
monster out of the deep which causes the death of Hippolyte.
Here is a clear instance of a supernatural intervention in human
affairs.

Yet there must be care in the way in which this is considered
before leaping to the conclusion that, by including it in his treatment of the subject, Racine is accepting that the gods play a part
in human affairs. What must be borne in mind is that the consequence of this supernatural action is by no means supernatural. Hippolyte dies, but this is in the order of nature. It was
precisely the reverse of this that Racine had not been able to accept in the dénouement of *Iphigenia in Aulis* of Euripides, and
was possibly the reason why he had not been able to write a
tragedy on the subject of *Alcestis*, which he had wanted to do.
Any intervention of the gods which upsets the order of nature
as, for instance, bringing the dead back to life, was not accept-
able. But the bringing about of an event by divine intervention
which could have been brought about by numerous natural
means is hardly a very convincing piece of evidence in support of
the case that *Phèdre* represents human beings as merely puppets

in the hands of superior forces who are controlling them. The way in which Hippolyte met his death was too well known, too much an accepted part of the legend, for it to be altered. It would seem that Racine felt able to keep this element of the story without committing himself to an absurdity as would have been the case had he adhered to the dénouement of *Iphigenia in Aulis.* Whatever may be the role of gods and goddesses in *Phèdre*, and this will have to be discussed, it is not that of directors of the action.

3. Moral Issues

Phèdre is a play written to be acted, which means that Racine cast his subject into a dramatic mould. What this signifies for the student of the play is that he must constantly bear in mind that the dramatic form demands a certain approach which is quite different from, say, the approach of the novelist. The way the dramatist uses the means at his disposal offers clues to his intentions which should not be ignored. An interesting aspect of *Phèdre* which can be used to illustrate this is the role of the confidant and the monologue in the play. These two devices, used by seventeenth-century dramatists to tell the audience the thoughts of the characters, among other things, are used in a rather special way in *Phèdre*. Théramène and Œnone are far from being conventional confidants. Both have definite parts to play in the unfolding of the action and both are given status. Théramène is Hippolyte's tutor and Œnone is Phèdre's nurse. Both are elderly and have been with their charges since birth. Both have opinions and offer advice, and both these opinions and advice provide a way of looking at what happens in the tragedy, which is an important ingredient in its interpretation. It is at the insistence of Œnone that Phèdre breaks her silence and reveals her secret, thus setting the tragedy in motion. For her to be able to exercise this kind of influence on Phèdre she must be given some kind of authority and her role must be filled out. We shall see how this is done when the development of the action of the play is considered. Similarly Théramène will be entrusted with recounting the death of Hippolyte. Such an important speech can have its full effect only in the mouth of someone who is more than a colourless confidant. Thus a dramatic device becomes significant because a playwright's approach to his subject is being revealed by the use he makes of it.

Similarly, the use of the monologue in *Phèdre* is not without interest. There are only four in *Phèdre*. Phèdre herself has two

(Act III, scene ii and Act IV, scene v) and Thésée has two (Act IV, scene iii and Act V, scene iv). Of these only the monologue of Phèdre in Act IV is a true monologue in which a character explores a state of mind. The others are linking scenes. One wonders why Racine did not use the monologue more in his presentation of *Phèdre*. It is true that Thierry Maulnier claims that many of Phèdre's speeches are monologues, that she is talking to herself rather than to her interlocutors on some occasions, but to say this is deliberately to ignore what Racine had done. It is worth asking whether the absence of monologues in *Phèdre* throws any light on Racine's way of looking at his subject. Is it possible that because of the nature of the dilemma with which Phèdre is faced the monologue would not be appropriate to express it? In his previous tragedies Racine had shown situations in which there are two sides; on the one hand the victims: Andromaque, Junie and Britannicus, Bérénice, Atalide and Bajazet, Monime, Iphigénie; on the other those who exercise power over the victims: Pyrrhus, Néron, Titus, Roxane, Mithridate and Agamemnon. Of course, these latter characters are, in another sense of the word, victims, but they have power, even though it proves useless to give them what they want. In these kinds of situations there is plenty of scope for the use of the monologue.

The situation of Phèdre does not fit into either of these categories. She is a victim who has no right to be a victim. She has power, but she cannot use it. She is torn, not between external forces, but within herself. Although this might seem to be ideal material for a monologue, Racine does not use it and the reason may be found in his interpretation of the role. To give Phèdre a monologue in which she argued with herself would be the equivalent of giving her a ticket of respectability. Her words may be recalled:

Je n'osais dans mes pleurs me noyer à loisir.
Je goûtais en tremblant ce funeste plaisir;
Et, sous un front serein déguisant mes alarmes,
Il fallait bien souvent me priver de mes larmes. (1247-50)

This indicates that Phèdre was not free to indulge in the luxury of a monologue in which she could give full expression to her sufferings. In the course of the play things do not change. Phèdre is faced with only one dilemma, has only one decision to make. She does not have to argue with herself about the nature of her passion for Hippolyte. She knows that it is wrong and no arguing can change that. The decision she has to take arises after the unexpected return of Thésée. What is she to do about the suggestion made by Œnone that she should take the initiative herself rather than wait to be accused? This could be the place for a monologue in which Phèdre argues with herself over the pros and cons of the case. Such a monologue would be intolerable, however, because it would at once introduce an element of reasoning into a decision which, if it is to be accepted at all, can only be accepted on the grounds that it is taken on the spur of the moment, and is not the result of reflection. Had Phèdre had the time to argue with herself, there can be hardly any doubt that she would never have consented to the accusation against Hippolyte being made. The question of Phèdre's responsibility is an important one and any clue that Racine gives us to help us to understand his intentions must be considered. Let us look for a moment at Phèdre from this point of view.

It has often been noted that the women characters in Racine's tragedies before *Phèdre* are of two types. There are the pure and innocent who love and are loved in return. Junie, Bérénice, Atalide, Monime and Iphigénie belong to this line of heroines. Their tragic situation springs from their threatened existence which is not going to allow them to enjoy the bliss which otherwise should be theirs. The other category consists of those women completely dominated by a passion for a man who does not love them in return. Hermione, Roxane and Eriphile belong in this category, and what charcterises them is that their passion allows no room for moral considerations and they are prepared to fight, to lie, to betray and to kill if this will help them to reach their goal. In Phèdre these two conceptions are united in the one individual. She is at one and the same time innocent and guilty, pure and impure, victim and tyrant. It follows from this that there must be a difference in the way in which Racine presents the tragedy of Phèdre, as internal forces rather than external forces are at work here, and the nature of the drama which arises from this must necessarily be different.

This draws our attention to an important aspect of *Phèdre* which determines the way the action unfolds. For the tragedy of Phèdre comes into existence when she speaks. Before the tragedy begins, if I can be allowed for a moment to postulate such a state of things, Phèdre is the only one who knows that she has fallen in love with Hippolyte. It is a secret hidden in her heart, and she intended to go to her grave without revealing it. In which case nothing would have happened. It is Œnone who persuades her to reveal the secret and once the secret is spoken, once the love is known, it assumes, so to speak, an existence of its own independent almost of Phèdre's will, and brings her to disaster. The dramatic problem facing Racine, therefore, is to create the situation in which the secret can be revealed and then further to create situations in which it can pursue its brief but catastrophic career. The way this is done will be considered below but, of course, it will turn on the conflict between the nature of Phèdre's passion and her attitude towards it.

Racine's conception of the passion of love, as illustrated in the tragedies which he had written before *Phèdre*, was that to be found in most of the novels and dramatic literature of the seventeenth century, not to mention the works of moralists like le père Le Moyne or philosophers like Descartes.[9] The existence of this overwhelming desire, taking possession of a human being to the exclusion of all other considerations rational or moral, was well documented. Its effects were similarly known, and the destruction of moral values, the abandonment of normal standards of behaviour, the degradation of the personality which resulted from it had all been described and illustrated in plays and novels. It is true that for the most part passion of this sort seemed to be the apanage of immoral people anyway so that there was no problem for them in giving full rein to their brutal desires. The moral were not immune from passion for those who did not love them in return. This tended, in the tragedies of

[9] I am thinking of the *Traité des passions de l'âme* published by Descartes in 1649 and the *Peintures morales* published by Le Moyne in 1640.

Racine, to be because the nature of the passion felt by the moral was different from that felt by the immoral. Or was it that passion unrequited had the effect of turning the moral into the immoral? It could be argued that this is what happens to Oreste in *Andromaque* who shows moral scruples when called upon to kill Pyrrhus at the behest of the woman he loves, Hermione. The only other character who would seem to fall into this category is Antiochus in *Bérénice*. This case is noteworthy because, as a character, he fails to convince. It would seem that those who do not give full rein to their passions because of their moral scruples are less dramatically interesting, and hence the sufferings of Antiochus are not appreciated.

The passion with which Racine endows Phèdre, or rather which he takes over from the sources he used, is the violent, all-consuming passion of an Hermione or Roxane. It is also adulterous and incestuous. It is the incestuous element that produces the horror in Phèdre herself, but the adulterous element must not be overlooked. Even if Hippolyte were not her stepson, Phèdre's passion was blameworthy from a moral point of view. There is no need to argue about the question of incest. Phèdre regards her passion as incestuous; in the world in which the events of the play take place it is incestuous. Therefore it is incestuous. It must be accepted that for the purposes of the play, Phèdre's passion is considered unnatural, and it is this unnaturalness which adds to the depth of meaning of the play. To what extent is Phèdre responsible for her passion? In one sense not at all. Her account of the way she fell in love with Hippolyte in Act I, scene iii is quite clear. Her falling in love with Hippolyte was an involuntary act and, therefore, beyond her control. Nevertheless, Phèdre *feels* responsible and this point must be underlined as it throws light on the whole conception of tragedy in the play. We are responsible for our own passions and our own bodies however much they may want to act independently of our will. It is this responsibility that Phèdre accepts. It does not seem to matter how we interpret Venus in this context. Racine transfers from Euripides (and other sources) the myth that Venus hated all the descendants of the sun because the sun is supposed to have discovered her illicit love affair with

Mars, and reported it to her husband. The myth provides a poetic framework in which the idea of passion and what it does can be expressed. Victims of passion are victims of forces which are superior to themselves.

Phèdre is such a victim, but the force springs from within herself. She recognises this and accepts the responsibility implied, so much so that she condemns herself simply for loving Hippolyte, although she has never tried to give a concrete reality to her love. She seeks remedies for her ill, but there is no remedy. She considers herself morally wrong even to think of loving Hippolyte and not loving her husband Thésée.

It may be as well to pause here a moment to consider standards. What are the standards of behaviour by which we are supposed to judge Phèdre? For the tragedy invites us to judge. Even if we put on one side Racine's preface to the play as being a piece of special pleading in which he is making claims for the moral value of the theatre which remind one of Molière defending *Tartuffe*, we must, nevertheless, be prepared to take a stand on right and wrong. Racine assumes such a stand in his spectators or readers. It is to be considered wrong to be incestuous; it is to be considered wrong to be adulterous. In the world where values like these are accepted, Phèdre is wrong. The wrongness, however, is not going to manifest itself in that way but in a different way. A false accusation is made against Hippolyte which results in his death. That this is wrong nobody can doubt. This is where the question of the responsibility of Phèdre becomes acute. To fall in love involuntarily is one thing; to tell lies is another. The wrongness of the one is thus given expression in the other. Phèdre bears responsibility for what happens to Hippolyte, and this is the terrible price that is paid for the release of the passion which had been under control. Everybody is destroyed by it in one way or another, and the destruction comes about because moral values have been destroyed. This may not seem completely relevant to the method Racine uses to present his subject dramatically, but in fact it determines the way in which the material is disposed and the way the audience is invited to look at the action of the play. This is the next point to be considered.

4. Questions of Structure

I want to look now at the way *Phèdre* is put together and to draw attention to some aspects of its structure which seem to me significant. On the one hand there are the mechanics of the play, the pieces of dramatic action which are fitted together and which enable the play to have a beginning, a middle and an end. These matters are determined by various considerations including the question of the three unities, *vraisemblance* and *bienséance*. Now Racine is widely admired for the skill with which he manages to put this machinery into operation, and rightly so, but nevertheless this admiration can sometimes direct attention to aspects of the structure of the play which are not of the first importance and ignore other, more fruitful approaches. Such approaches were those practised by Mauron, Goldmann and Barthes and provoked much controversy[10]. Whilst it must be admitted that these critics have exaggerated much, overlooked much, taken too much for granted and made assertions impossible to prove, the fact remains that it is no longer possible not to take into account some of what they have got to say. The main advantage, to my mind, of considering the views of these critics is that they force us to examine our interpretation of Racine's concept of tragedy in ways that would not have occurred to us and even if we reject some of the wilder assertions, we are still left with much which is worthwhile. I shall comment on some points where they seem to me to be relevant to aspects of *Phèdre* in their place.

Here I would like to look at what I have called the mechanics of the play. It is no part of my purpose to decry the skills of Racine in putting a play together, but sometimes it is necessary, in order to make the point that Racine was fitting a subject to a

[10] This controversy has now died down and it is possible to take a reasonably balanced view of the contribution made by the *nouvelle critique* to the study of Racinian tragedy.

form, to show that the form was made to give way and yield if required to do so by the exigencies of the subject. Let us look at *Phèdre* bearing this in mind. The first thing to be noted is that no reason is given why the play begins when it does. Many of Racine's plays begin with the announcement that something special marks the day which has been chosen. An outsider arrives, and this provides the trigger which sparks off the action inherent in a dangerous situation (*Andromaque*). A piece of news can have the same effect (*Mithridate, Iphigénie*) or a decision has been taken, or is about to be taken, which will affect people's lives (*Britannicus, Bérénice*). None of this is true of *Phèdre*. The unexpected event which marks the day on which the action happens is the return of Thésée after his death had been announced. This does not, however, happen at the beginning of the play, nor is it the trigger which sets the play in motion. The two events which start the play are the decision which Hippolyte announces to Théramène that he is going away from Trézène, and the revelation by Phèdre to Œnone of the secret malady which is driving her to her death. These are two quite separate actions which are linked together only because Racine wishes them to be so linked. Neither is any reason given why these events should take place at this particular moment. Then comes the announcement that Thésée is dead, an announcement made precisely at the moment when, after years of silence, Phèdre reveals her love for Hippolyte to Œnone. Nothing could be more convenient or less *vraisemblable* or so it would seem. Yet this is not what *vraisemblance* is, and the point is worth making. *Vraisemblance* is not concerned with the mechanics of the drama which is being discussed here, but with much wider issues of human behaviour. The reason why Racine uses this device is, of course, to make possible the two declarations of love which constitute the main business of Act II. The first two acts are, therefore, built first on nothing, so to speak, then on a report which turns out to be false. What conclusions can be drawn from this? I think that it is possible to surprise Racine, the dramatist, at work.

I have said that *Phèdre* is a tragedy the action of which depends on the breaking of silence by Phèdre herself. It is essential for the tragedy to be set in motion that Phèdre reveal her secret. So the tragedy must begin with this happening, and Racine follows the pattern of his predecessors, Euripides and Seneca, in doing this. One of the opening scenes therefore must show Phèdre revealing her secret, and the scene which Racine writes follows quite closely that of Euripides, as we shall see. But it is not the first scene of the play. The first scene of the play shows us Hippolyte revealing, or not quite revealing, a secret which concerns love. Similarly, in Act II, the scene in which Phèdre declares her love to Hippolyte is preceded by a scene in which Hippolyte declares his love to Aricie. This parallelism in the way *Phèdre* is constructed has, of course, often been noted and must not be overlooked. Racine makes some specific dramatic points by arranging his material in this way. What is less often noted, however, is that the treatment of Hippolyte's scenes must have been suggested by the Phèdre scenes. That is to say, the scene in which Phèdre reveals her secret to Œnone is the fixed point. This scene existed, or one like it, in Euripides and in Seneca, and Racine uses it as the starting point of his tragedy. So by choosing to place Hippolyte in a similar situation Racine is deliberately making the Phèdre scene throw its shadow before in order, presumably, to get the effect of parallelism which he wants. Thus the treatment of Hippolyte in the first scene of the play is determined by the treatment of Phèdre in the first scene in which she appears which, in turn, is determined by the source.

The theme, then seems to be the important factor in shaping the way the dramatic action is going to be presented, and the theme here is of secrets being told, or rather of those who have secrets being persuaded to reveal them. This is what takes precedence over mere mechanical devices, and *Phèdre* illustrates this wonderfully. At the end of Act II a report is brought that Thésée is alive, and Act III confirms the truth of this report, and Thésée appears. The consequences of this event are the false accusations made against Hippolyte by Œnone, sanctioned by Phèdre, and the cursing of Hippolyte by Thésée. These events fill the first two scenes of Act IV and, clearly, move the action forward. The rest of that act is, however, filled with the scenes of jealousy when Phèdre learns of Hippolyte's love for Aricie.

The events, of course, are linked together, as is easily shown. Once again, though, Racine subordinates the mechanics of the drama to the situation which he wishes to bring into existence. It is clear, for instance, that when Thésée says at the end of scene iv:

> Je vais moi-même encore au pied de ses autels
> Le presser d'accomplir ses serments immortels. (1191-92)

a device is being used to remove him from the stage so that the jealousy scene can proceed. Similar comments can be made about Act V. The death of Hippolyte which, because of *bienséance* and the unity of place, must happen elsewhere, is the main action of this act. What we actually see on the stage is, first, a scene between Hippolyte and Aricie which neither aids nor retards this dénouement but, in fact, introduces an element of the unreal because Hippolyte does not leave the stage until line 1140, and his death will have taken place before the return of Théramène to recount it at line 1488. This telescoping of time has not passed unnoticed by critics. It shows how futile it is to try and tie Racine down to exact limits. He uses time as he uses the other ingredients of drama — to suit his purposes. Where, as here, it is the event that counts and not the time it takes to happen, then interest is concentrated on the event and the time is left undefined. When time is relevant, it is brought forward and emphasised; otherwise not.

5. *Opening Scenes*

The play opens with a scene between Hippolyte and Théramène.
The first scene of any play must deal with the facts which it is
necessary for the audience to know if the action is to be
understood. We need to know who is talking and why. We need
to know the situation and the relationships which exist between
the various people whom we see or whom we hear mentioned. In
this first scene of *Phèdre* all of this is done. We learn that we are
in Trézène. In the course of the conversation between Hippolyte
and Théramène, the names of Phèdre, Thésée and Aricie are all
brought in and we learn facts about them. Phèdre is Hippolyte's
stepmother and is mortally ill with a disease the nature of which
she refuses to reveal. Thésée has been absent for six months and
his whereabouts are not known. Aricie, the invented character,
needs rather more introduction than the others so her *état civil* is
spelt out by Théramène:

> Jamais l'aimable sœur des cruels Pallantides
> Trempa-t-elle aux complots de ses frères perfides?
>
> (53-54)

Pallas and Aegeus (Egée), who was the father of Thésée, were
the sons of Pandion king of Athens, but the sons of Pallas
claimed that Egée was only the adopted child of Pandion (a
claim upheld by Hippolyte (II.ii.497)) and that therefore their
claim to the throne of Athens was stronger than that of their
cousin Thésée. It was for this reason that Thésée fought and
killed the sons of Pallas, fifty in number according to
mythology, but six according to Racine. Aricie's claim to the
throne of Athens is then a strong one in that she is the only true
descendant of Pandion. For this reason Thésée had forbidden
her to marry.

These dynastic details may seem tedious, but the political

background of *Phèdre* is too often neglected, and it has a part to play in the unfolding of the tragedy. Aricie, as an invented character, is provided with a well-authenticated family history which has the double function of placing her firmly in the network of relationships in which all the characters of *Phèdre* are involved, and to make her forbidden fruit as far as Hippolyte is concerned. For the relationship between Hippolyte and Aricie is the subject of this first scene. Hippolyte announces that he is leaving Trézène, and Théramène tries to find the reason for this departure. The resulting conversation is used to give the information already mentioned, but more than that it is used to create an atmosphere and to establish the background of fable which serves as scenery, so to speak, for the play.

What the exact place is in which the events of the tragedy occur is not clear. 'La scène est à Trézène, ville du Péloponnèse' is the only indication given. Are we, for instance, indoors or outdoors? When Phèdre comes to see the light at the beginning of the third scene, is she emerging from the palace onto a terrace, or is she simply coming from some inner, darkened room into one flooded with the morning sun? Sea and sky are at hand as constant reference is made to both, but it is not clear whether they can be seen nor is it necessary that they should be. Individual producers of the play will determine what they want from that point of view. What Racine does is to create a background that demands the use of the imagination. In *Phèdre* this is of two kinds. There is the physical evocation of Greece, its islands and the Mediterranean. Athens, Corinth, Sparta, Crete, Argos, Epirus are mentioned at different times in the play and these names provide a firm geographical location, invested with an aura of magic by the means Racine uses to describe them. Athens, for instance, becomes:

Les superbes remparts que Minerve a bâtis (360)

and the description invites the imagination to go to work. So the field of action of *Phèdre* embraces a large area in which some events have occurred in the past, some are occurring and some may occur in the future. This area is also the field of action of

the great myths of Greece, and this leads to the second point
about background. All the characters whom Racine paints in
Phèdre have an ancestry which links them to these myths. Aricie
and Thésée are descended, as we have seen, from Pandion,
himself descended from Erectheus (Erechthée), child of the
earth. Through his mother, Thésée is descended from Pittheus
(Pitthée) who is descended from Zeus. Phèdre is 'la fille de
Minos et de Pasiphaé' which links her to Zeus (through Minos)
and to the sun (through Pasiphaé) descended from the earth and
the sky. Hippolyte being the son of Thésée had, of course, the
same ancestry as he has, while through his mother, Antiope, an
Amazon, is descended from Ares, the god of war. Therefore all
these people are supposedly linked to the elemental forces, the
earth, the sky, the sun. The sea plays its part by the intervention
of Neptune, brother of Zeus.

What importance does all this have for *Phèdre*? It provides
the material on which the poetic imagination of Racine went to
work with such marvellously evocative results. It plays on the
sensibility of the spectator or reader weaving magical threads for
him to follow. It widens and deepens the significance of what is
being described by adding suggestiveness to factual things. It
provides an elaborate, metaphorical framework which reflects,
on a universal scale, human activities. In short, it supplies the
scenery that Racine was unable to supply any other way. The
necessity of observing the unity of place becomes, therefore, the
raison d'être of one of the most fertile sources of powerful
dramatic effects which, in the hands of the great poet that
Racine was, created so much that is remarkable in *Phèdre*. The
conversation between Hippolyte and Théramène in this first
scene offers many examples of this kind of thing. Consider, for
instance, part of the speech in which Hippolyte is talking about
his father:

> Quand tu me dépeignais ce héros intrépide
> Consolant les mortels de l'absence d'Alcide,
> Les monstres étouffés et les brigands punis,
> Procuste, Cercyon, et Scirron, et Sinnis,
> Et les os dispersés du géant d'Epidaure,

> Et la Crète fumant du sang du Minotaure.
> Mais, quand tu récitais des faits moins glorieux,
> Sa foi partout offerte et reçue en cent lieux;
> Hélène à ses parents dans Sparte dérobée;
> Salamine témoin des pleurs de Péribée... (77-86)

These proper names bring to life the fabulous past of Thésée, recalling his deeds of valour and his deeds of love and, in so doing, striking notes which set up reverberations which do not die away quickly: Alcide, Minotaure, Hélène. Such names cannot be pronounced, especially with the musical accompaniment that Racine gives them:

> Consolant les mortels de l'absence d'Alcide

or:

> Salamine témoin des pleurs de Péribée

without echoes being set in motion which create the atmosphere of poetic magic in which the whole play is bathed.

I have noted two aspects of this first scene, that which consists in providing information and that which consists in providing atmosphere and background. It remains to look at the content of the scene insofar as it sets the action of the play in motion. The scene is built on the idea that a young man in love behaves in a certain way and that a respectful son behaves in a certain way. Hippolyte is both of these. He is in love and he regrets that he is in love because his love is contrary to his father's wishes. That Racine was departing from the conventional portrait of Hippolyte is, of course, evident. Why he did it has often been discussed, but there seems no reason not to believe Racine when he says in his preface:

> J'ai cru lui devoir donner quelque faiblesse qui le rendrait
> un peu coupable envers son père, sans pourtant lui rien
> ôter de cette grandeur d'âme avec laquelle il épargne l'hon-
> neur de Phèdre et se laisse opprimer sans l'accuser. J'ap-

pelle faiblesse la passion qu'il ressent malgré lui pour
Aricie, qui est la fille et la sœur des ennemis mortels de son
père.

For Racine the hero of a tragedy should not be exempt from imperfection, and in this he is following Aristotle.

The nature and the extent of the flaw is open to question and
different ages may have different opinions on the subject. That
Hippolyte himself regards his love as a fault allows Racine to
present that love in a certain way, and he thus reconciles his concept of a tragic hero with the demands of the subject. Love is
seen as a battle. Aricie is 'une ennemie' from whom Hippolyte is
fleeing. He does not want to have to assume the 'joug' (to which
Thésée has had to submit himself so many times) and admit that
he has succumbed to a 'vainqueur'. This imagery of war will be
used frequently in *Phèdre* and not least by Phèdre herself. Com-
monplace and cliché-like metaphorical language thus assumes
the full vigour of its meaning. Aricie is an enemy, literally, of
Thésée and his family. It may have even been this fact,
Théramène suggests interestingly, that made Hippolyte fall in
love with her:

> Thésée ouvre vos yeux, en voulant les fermer;
> Et sa haine, irritant une flamme rebelle,
> Prête à son ennemie une grâce nouvelle. (116-18)

Hippolyte as a lover, is not typical of his kind and does not
behave as such. In order to try and come to terms with the two
conflicting emotions which are dominating him, his love for
Aricie and his dutiful respect for his father, he sees only one
solution, to go away, to avoid Aricie. This is the decision he now
announces to Théramène and it at once sets the tone of the
tragedy. Something is wrong at Trézène. The woods and forests
no longer ring with the shouts of Hippolyte and Théramène on
their hunting expeditions, no longer can a chariot be seen racing
along the shore or the struggles of a horse being tamed. There is
a secret, a secret more than half guessed, but a secret nevertheless, and there is more than one secret being kept at Trézène.

How well Racine, therefore, contrives to create in this first scene the atmosphere appropriate to the subject. The essence of a secret is that it should not be told. This scene shows attempts being made to discover the secret, and the dramatic interest arises from the tension between the two speakers as they spar with each other. *Phèdre* is going to be a tragedy resulting from a secret told that ought never to have been told, of words spoken that ought never to have been spoken. This secret, when revealed, assumes a monstrous existence of its own, as it were, which will destroy both those who told and those who listened. It is appropriate, therefore, that the opening scenes of the play should deal with the theme of secrets and that thus a note is struck suitable to the tragedy that is about to unfold.

6. Phèdre

We can now turn to the question of Phèdre herself. How does Racine present her in the tragedy? What is the significance of the scenes which he writes for her? How do we interpret her role? What are the implications of what she does? These questions suggest an approach which may prove fruitful. There are several points to be borne in mind as the investigation progresses. One, for instance, an obvious one, is the use Racine made of his sources. Seeking sources for sources' sake is not rewarding but the changes an author makes in his use of a source can be illuminating. The point is immediately of relevance as the very first scene in which Phèdre appears has, as has already been noted, a counterpart in the *Hippolytus* of Euripides. Racine follows the main line of the scene in Euripides but his emphasis is different. What emerges clearly in Racine's treatment of this episode is that he uses the indications given in Euripides to show that Phèdre no longer feels herself a part of the world of other people. Her love for Hippolyte is her reality, but it is an impossible reality. Hence her feeling of alienation from all that surrounds her. This is what Racine brings out so strongly in this scene, and it initiates his interpretation of Phèdre's role.

Œnone interrupts the farewells of Hippolyte and Théramène to announce the imminent arrival of Phèdre who wants to see daylight once more before leaving it for ever. The part played by the imagery of light and darkness, of day and night, of white and black, in *Phèdre* is nearly always emphasised in discussions of the play. I do not propose to develop this point except at those stages of the tragedy where, it seems to me, some significance can be attached to the imagery which illuminates the meaning of the tragedy. This does not seem to be the case here. Phèdre coming out of the darkness into the light is so obvious that no commentary is necessary. However, let us note her first words:

> N'allons point plus avant, demeurons, chère Œnone
> (153)

This suggests that the place that has been reached is not necessarily the place which might have been reached: 'N'allons point plus avant', let us stop here, we may not have reached the ideal place but this will do, a resting place, a stage on a journey. This is what is suggested by these words, and the suggestion is an interesting one because it makes us think that the spot chosen by Racine has no particular significance except that it is somewhere between a point of departure and a point of arrival but is neither of those places. It might be worth recalling what Barthes has to say about *le lieu racinien* at this point.[11] He sees three sections in what he calls *l'espace racinien*, *la Chambre*, *l'Anti-Chambre* and *l'Extérieur*. In the *Chambre* is the 'lieu invisible et redoutable où la Puissance est tapie'; *l'Anti-Chambre* is the 'lieu d'attente et par conséquant site théâtral obligé' which is between the space where decisions are taken and the third space *l'Extérieur* where things happen. The *Extérieur* itself is divided into three sections: *celui du rêve de fuite, celui de l'événement, celui de la mort.*

How does this help in the present instance? By drawing our attention to a way of looking at the action which we otherwise might not have considered. We become aware of the transitoriness of the moment that is before us and of the place that we see. The individuals are caught briefly and held for our attention for a moment, but their lives are really being played out elsewhere. What we see, as symbolised by the negativeness of the place where they are, is only a temporary resting place from which they look back or forward to other places, in some cases more desirable, in others less so, where they could be. Life is not being lived where we see it; it is being lived elsewhere, and if it is better and more desirable, then it is being sought. Alternatively, the attempt may be to escape from what is in there, behind, and there is a pause for a moment on the way out to give expression to these things. If we think of this we can see how well it applies to Phèdre at this point. Dying 'd'un mal qu'elle s'obstine à taire' (45), her life has been dominated by her secret for years, hidden

11 See Barthes (*20*) pp.17-20 and passim.

away but the source of frenzied activity nevertheless. This was the reality of her existence, harsh, unbearable, full of suffering and tears shed in secret. Her dream, her would-be reality is the world in which she and Hippolyte could be lovers, an impossible dream but one for which she yearns:

> Dieux! que ne suis-je assise à l'ombre des forêts!
> Quand pourrai-je, au travers d'une noble poussière,
> Suivre de l'œil un char fuyant dans la carrière? (176-78)

With what subtlety Racine uses a hint from Euripides, who paints Phèdre as wanting to go hunting, to convey this sense of alienation from reality which is what characterises Phèdre in this first part of the scene. Her secret world, her *Chambre* in a sense, is the world of her impossible love from which she is trying to escape by death. That this is so is shown by the remarkable change that she undergoes once the secret is revealed. Clear, articulate, fluent, she recounts the history of her passion for Hippolyte in a way that contrasts strongly with what has gone before, the broken phrases, the half-expressed ideas, the vague references, the invocations. As her secret world of love and shame and guilt is given expression, it is assuming an existence, which it has always had for Phèdre, of its own.

Let us look a little more closely at the opening of this scene. Phèdre, on the point of death, has dragged herself out to the light to see it once more before she dies. Why is Phèdre in this state? Because of her sense of guilt? To Œnone's question:

> Vos mains n'ont point trempé dans le sang innocent
> (220)

she replies:

> Grâces au ciel, mes mains ne sont point criminelles.
> Plût aux dieux que mon cœur fût innocent comme elles!
> (221-22)

Phèdre is thus presented to us straight away as a woman who

considers herself guilty of a crime although she has done nothing deserving that name. What she has done is to fall in love with her stepson but nobody knows that except herself. Her love is for her a crime although it must also be borne in mind that her suffering comes from the frustration caused by passion that cannot be assuaged. She expresses her sense of horror of what has happened to her by her evocation of her mother and her sister in unforgettable phrases:

> Ô haine de Vénus! Ô fatale colère!
> Dans quels égarements l'amour jeta ma mère! (249-50)

and:

> Ariane, ma soeur, de quel amour blessée,
> Vous mourûtes aux bords où vous fûtes laissée! (253-54)

Love has been for them either a crime or a source of suffering. Of the three she considers that she is the most wretched:

> Puisque Vénus le veut, de ce sang déplorable
> Je péris la dernière et la plus misérable. (257-58)

Thus the sense of guilt is very strong. Why is this so? Is Phèdre in Péguy's famous phrase: 'une janséniste à qui la grâce a manqué'? To consider her so is both to add unnecessary overtones to the interpretation of Phèdre's tragedy and to subtract from its essentially human source. Phèdre has fallen in love because she is a human being and human beings do fall in love. It is her tragedy that this love is directed where it is impossible that it can be ever fulfilled. Still this is not a crime. Love is involuntary, or can be, and is it fair that Phèdre should be held responsible for what happens to her? This is where the present scene is interesting because it is justified by what happens subsequently. Phèdre is right to feel guilty because her love, when given the opportunity to express itself, proves that it is indeed a catastrophic and destructive force which, when released, is beyond control. What happens in *Phèdre* is the demonstration of the crime which

Phèdre carries within her. And it is inevitable that it should be so. She is thus condemned as she condemns herself because her humanity has made her a source of evil.

Several things are remarkable in this speech in which Phèdre recounts her love for Hippolyte and its history. The physical nature of the passion is brought out:

> Athènes me montra mon superbe ennemi:
> Je le vis, je rougis, je pâlis à sa vue;
> Un trouble s'éleva dans mon âme éperdue;
> Mes yeux ne voyaient plus, je ne pouvais parler;
> Je sentis tout mon corps et transir et brûler. (272-76)

These symptoms of passion were well known in the seventeenth century, and were used to indicate violent sexual feelings. The *bienséances* prevented Racine from being explicit in describing Phèdre's passion, but the suggestiveness with which he replaces direct expression is, in itself, more effective in conveying his meaning:

> Quand ma bouche implorait le nom de la déesse,
> J'adorais Hippolyte; et, le voyant sans cesse,
> Même au pied des autels que je faisais fumer,
> J'offrais tout à ce dieu que je n'osais nommer.
> Je l'évitais partout. Ô comble de misère!
> Mes yeux le retrouvaient dans les traits de son père.
> (285-90)

This is the all-invading passion that Phèdre tries to control. Her speech goes on to tell how she did this. She used her reason to act a part, that of the unjust stepmother and is successful to the extent that Hippolyte is banished. Then she goes on to say:

> Mes jours moins agités coulaient dans l'innocence (298)

and she pursued her life as wife of Thésée.

Here we pause to question the time span involved. How long ago did all this take place? How long has this passion lasted?

There has been time for Phèdre to bear children and, indeed, to start bringing them up. It must be a question of years. How long between Hippolyte's banishment and Phèdre's arrival in Trézène? We know how long Thésée has been away, something over six months (line 5) which is presumably the length of time Phèdre has been in Trézène. These questions are worth asking only for the purpose of alerting us to the use of time by Racine. It would be absurd to pretend that we are dealing here with a series of events that can be given specific existence in time, as though these things had actually happened and could be dated. What is happening in this speech is that Racine is showing how the past nourishes the present. The past is of interest in that it intrudes into the present and makes its presence felt. The present is what it is because the past has made it so, and the fleeting moment of the present is given substantiation by the past. Thus, whether it is a question of years, months or days is hardly relevant. To attempt to put a calendar on these events is to distort the vision which Racine is creating. This is one of the marvels of his use of the three unities. Instead of using them to tie himself down to a specific moment or place, he uses them to liberate himself from these constraints and move his dramatic action to much vaster planes.

Finally, in this speech there are the references to Venus, one of which is the famous:

> Ce n'est plus une ardeur dans mes veines cachée:
> C'est Vénus tout entière à sa proie attachée. (305-6)

The role of the gods in *Phèdre* has already been discussed and what has been said holds good for this speech. Venus represents the irrational force at work in Phèdre and is a convenient way of referring to it. There is not space to develop the point here but the relationships between gods and men in *Phèdre*, if we were to assume the existence of separate, supernatural beings with the power to influence men's actions, show a very odd state of affairs. When Phèdre prays to Venus what does she pray for? To be released from her influence? But Venus hates chastity which is why, in Euripides, she is supposed to have hated Hippolytus.

By falling in love with Hippolyte, it could be argued, Phèdre is paying homage to Venus and hardly needs to build temples to her. Her love is temple enough. This is, however, to attempt to apply logic in a field where logic has no place to be, but it is not, I think, without its use as it leads us, surely, to an understanding of what is really meant, a metaphor, an image, a poetic way of describing those forces which wreak such havoc in human beings. Phèdre does not try to shuffle off her responsibility for her passion on to a malevolent Deity but accepts it as part of the price to be paid for being in the world. The sense of shame and guilt which characterises Phèdre in the earlier part of the scene continues throughout the speech. She is racked with horror because of the adulterous and incestuous nature of the love she feels for Hippolyte. It is 'une flamme si noire', and the daring combination of noun and adjective underline that nature of the unnatural passion which possesses her. The only escape is death, the 'out there' for which she is striving, given that the realisation of her impossible dream will never come about. She reveals her secret to Œnone because she is on the verge of death. The irony is that in a very short time she will be dead but in that short space, short because of the relentless unity of time, which constitutes the last day of her life, she will live and suffer more intensely than ever before and in such a way that all she strove to do to preserve what she calls her 'gloire', and which can be thought of as what she is in the world, her position, her influence, her reputation, everything which gives her her own place in the world of men, will be irrevocably destroyed and reduced to nothing. Her meaning as a human being will be gone and she will have to face this in all its horror. Our purpose now is to see how this is brought about as the action of the tragedy progresses.

News is brought that Thésée is dead. Already others are rushing into action to cope with the situation. If the king of Athens is dead the question of his successor arises. The city is even now trying to decide the issue. Is it to be Phèdre's son (and, therefore, Phèdre who would act as regent in such a case), Hippolyte or Aricie, whose claim is a strong one? Hippolyte himself is already making preparations to set off for Athens to see what the situation is. On the surface, therefore, the politics of power are in operation. In Racine, however, power is of use for one purpose only: to further the personal desires of those who hold it. Power is a weapon to be used in the pursuit of the satisfaction of passion. All the characters will use it in this way. Phèdre will use it, or think of using it, to tempt Hippolyte. Hippolyte will use it to further his cause with Aricie, handing over to her the throne of Athens. Would he have done that had he not been in love with her? Even Œnone will use it, in a sense, to bring Phèdre back from the brink of the grave by using the specious argument:

> Votre flamme devient une flamme ordinaire;
> Thésée en expirant vient de rompre les nœuds
> Qui faisaient tout le crime et l'horreur de vos feux.
>
> (350-52)

Had the secret not been told, Phèdre would not have had to listen to such blandishments but the secret has been told and the tragedy is beginning. The past is now going to make its ravages in the present, but in a present which is not really a present, since the news of Thésée's death is false. Even while it is being broadcast he is on his way back, and will soon arrive in Trézène. In the short space of time, this false time when things seem to be different from what they really are, irrevocable things will have been said (and in the terms of Racinian tragedy that means *done*) that will ensure that all, Phèdre, Hippolyte, Thésée and Aricie will come to disaster.

The device of using false news of a death had already been used by Racine in *Mithridate* and was, indeed, fairly commonly used in seventeenth-century French tragedy. Had he not used this device Racine would not have been able to treat his subject. The death of Thésée is to *Phèdre* what Eriphile was to *Iphigénie*: a means of overcoming an obstacle which would otherwise have made the subject dramatically unworkable. His use of it is very subtle. The news of the death of Thésée permits the development of the action in an imaginary period of time, time that does not really exist because its existence depends on an event which has not taken place. To Phèdre and to Hippolyte is given the opportunity of trying to realise their dream but because, in this world, dreams of this kind are rarely realised it is not a matter of wonder that later on the illusion is shattered and that harsh reality makes its reappearance. Thus the false news of the death of Thésée, far from being a crude device, is used by Racine to explore what happens when prospects of dream-worlds coming true betray human beings into believing that things can be other than they are.

The second act is the act of declarations. Again Racine uses the same technique that he had used in Act I. Phèdre's scene of declaration is preceded by that of Hippolyte to Aricie. The effect of this is that the spectator knows, at the outset of the scene between Phèdre and Hippolyte, that the obstacle that separates them is even greater than Phèdre knows.

The news that Thésée is dead releases the pent-up passions of both Hippolyte and Phèdre. Both rush to be with their beloved, not with the intention of telling them that they are loved, but simply to see them. Both have excuses. Hippolyte is going to tell Aricie that he proposes to make her Queen of Athens, while Phèdre wishes to seek the protection of Hippolyte for her children. The two scenes follow similar lines of development but, of course, with completely different outcomes. The act begins, however, by introducing us to Aricie, and it is worth noting the picture that is presented of her. Let us not forget that this scene, as the ones that follow, shows the characters in a fairy-tale world, a world that really does not exist, a world in which Thésée is dead. For Aricie it is like a dream, a dream so blissful that she can hardly believe it:

Ismène, dis-tu vrai? N'es-tu point abusée? (369)

Ismène, playing the role that confidantes always play, that of believing what seems obvious and what seems to solve all problems, assures her that she can indulge her dream — which Aricie proceeds to do, and in so doing recounts her history.

We are given a picture of what Aricie represents. She is one in that line of Racinian heroines who are victims, cut off from their past and in a hostile and dangerous world in which they feel themselves threatened. Andromaque represents the most developed of these figures but Junie, Monime and Eriphile also fall into this category. There is a particular pathos about this kind of situation which Racine exploits to the full. Aricie describes her love for Hippolyte, and Racine takes care to distinguish it from the passion of Phèdre. The love of Aricie is not based solely on the physical attractions of Hippolyte, as she makes clear:

> J'aime, je prise en lui de plus nobles richesses (441)

These two conceptions of love, the one a purely physical attraction and the other based on a recognition of the noble qualities of the one loved, run throughout Racine's tragedies and are nowhere brought into sharper relief than here. One can wonder how valid the concept is, but Racine is following a well-established tradition in postulating the existence of these two kinds of love or passion. The purpose it serves is to show different planes of activity. Aricie and Hippolyte are on that noble plane where humanity attempts to act heroically. Aricie too thinks of love in warlike terms. She sees Hippolyte as an enemy to be conquered and the more worthy to be conquered in that his defences aginst love have hitherto been impregnable. It is in war that heroism is achieved, so the characters representing heroic values think in these terms.

The Aricie-Hippolyte theme in *Phèdre* serves, among other things, as a standard of moral behaviour against which aberrations from such standards can be measured. The declaration scene between Hippolyte and Aricie is based on these moral values and yet still follows the psychology of love as interpreted by Racine. Hippolyte is now king of Trézène. He intends to make Aricie queen of Athens. Crete will be for Phèdre's son. How noble it all sounds!

> Je pars, et vais, pour vous,
> Réunir tous les vœux partagés entre nous. (507-8)

The reason behind it, however, is love, not a disinterested wish to be of service to Aricie. From the expression of gratitude by Aricie to an outburst from Hippolyte is but a short step. Racine's technique is to develop the conversation along the lines he wants by using words which will act as triggers to release emotions. Thus Aricie says to Hippolyte:

> N'était-ce pas assez de ne me point haïr?
> Et d'avoir si longtemps pu défendre votre âme
> De cette inimitié... (516-18)

Inimitié and *haïr* are dangerous words to use to young men full of love, and so it proves in this case. When the talk has turned to what they feel for each other, how can the temptation be resisted to talk of love? Hippolyte cannot and does not. His declaration of love is full of charm and has a haunting quality which is not sufficiently recognised, and it merits quotation:

> Depuis près de six mois, honteux, désespéré
> Portant partout le trait dont je suis déchiré,
> Contre vous, contre moi, vainement je m'éprouve:
> Présente, je vous fuis; absente, je vous trouve;
> Dans le fond des forêts votre image me suit;
> La lumière du jour, les ombres de la nuit,
> Tout retrace à mes yeux les charmes que j'évite;
>
> Tout vous livre à l'envi le rebelle Hippolyte.
> Moi-même, pour tout fruit de mes soins superflus,
> Maintenant je me cherche, et ne me trouve plus. (539-48)

This is the way of expressing love, we are told later on, by one who is not used to talking this kind of language. From this we can assume that Hippolyte's declaration of love does not follow the usual pattern of these things. Hippolyte's declaration of love to Aricie can be compared with Phèdre's account to Œnone in Act I of her falling in love with Hippolyte. There is a similarity in the way that each analyses what has happened to him or her. Love obliges Hippolyte to look into himself and to understand that he, too, is

Asservi maintenant sous la commune loi (535)

There are no privileged beings in the world of Racine. Just as Phèdre is the victim of her humanity, so Hippolyte has to come to terms with the fact that he cannot escape the consequences of being a man. He has rebelled against this law but is now obliged to recognise that there is no rule which exempts him. Hence the confusion, the uncertainty which is expressed in the lines above with their haunting quality:

Contre vous, contre moi, vainement je m'éprouve:
Présente, je vous fuis; absente, je vous trouve (541-42)

The same obsession which tortured Phèdre:

Je l'évitais partout. Ô comble de misère!
Mes yeux le retrouvaient dans les traits de son père.
(289-90)

here is described by Hippolyte. Unlike Phèdre, however, Hippolyte will not have to pursue the path of self-knowledge to its ultimate catastrophic conclusion. He has brushed against the unknown that lurks within himself:

Maintenant je me cherche, et ne me trouve plus (548)

but, fortunately for him, will not have to progress further along this path. His love is reciprocated and he can, therefore, turn his eyes back from these unknown regions and regain his equilibrium. The course of his tragedy will be in a different direction.

Hippolyte is by no means a conventional sighing lover nor is Aricie a conventional counterpart. As always Racine has taken convention and used it to make suggestions about human beings and their relationships which go far beyond the superficial description of a banal love affair.

It is time to turn to the great scene v of Act II, the scene between Phèdre and Hippolyte. It is in this scene that Racine displays clearly the nature of the passion which Phèdre feels for Hippolyte. The sensuality which forms so great a part of this passion is brought out in full measure, and all is done without overstepping the boundaries laid down by *bienséance*. Let us recall what has to be done. Phèdre is fascinated, obsessed, magnetised by Hippolyte. Obliged to show the full extent of this obsession without indecency, Racine, by the very force of the imaginative means he used, succeeded in writing a scene which is more full of sensuality than would have been possible had he been able to use all the freedom available to playwrights of later ages. The scene has a counterpart in Seneca's tragedy, and Racine borrowed at least one idea from that scene, the passage where Phèdre talks of going with Thésée into the labyrinth, but otherwise the two scenes are quite different. In Seneca, Phaedra is determined to make an effort to seduce Hippolytus. In Racine there is no such intention but rather a gradual abandonment of all the defences which Phèdre had so painfully and elaborately built up. For it must be remembered that by telling Hippolyte that she loves him, Phèdre is going to have to cross an enormous obstacle. She is going to have to overcome all the inhibitions and taboos which prevent a woman from telling a man that she loves him. Not only does that stand in her way but also her relationship to Hippolyte, as the wife (or widow as she thinks at the moment) of his father.

There is a great barrier to be crossed and it is instructive to see how Racine copes with the problem. It is as though there were a precipice into which Phèdre is going to fall. She gets closer and closer to the edge, draws back but goes forward again until she gets too near and falls over. An understanding of this scene which sees Hippolyte as having guessed what Phèdre is trying to say before she actually says it seems to me to be mistaken. Hippolyte, in his replies, is trying to make polite conversation; he is, if anything, bored and uninterested, and wants to bring the interview to a close as soon as possible. Phèdre draws near the precipice for the first time when she says:

> Que dis-je? Il n'est point mort, puisqu'il respire en vous.
> Toujours devant mes yeux je crois voir mon époux:

Je le vois, je lui parle; et mon cœur... je m'égare,
Seigneur; ma folle ardeur malgré moi se déclare. (627-30)

She pulls herself up short in time, but Hippolyte's well-meant words of comfort only serve to spark off a fresh outburst. In the same way that the word *inimitié* had been the trigger that had set Hippolyte off, so *embrasée* (633) fulfils the same function here:

Oui, prince, je languis, je brûle pour Thésée. (634)

is Phèdre's response, picking up the idea of burning inherent in Hippolyte's *embrasée*. This line introduces Phèdre's famous labyrinth speech. Phèdre uses her imagination to construct a picture in which she sees herself leading Thésée/Hippolyte into the labyrinth and either perishing with him there or returning with him to safety and, presumably, happiness. Is it necessary to give a Freudian interpretation to this passage as Martin Turnell does? I hardly think so. Such an interpretation adds nothing to the meaning of the scene and, indeed, distracts the attention from what is really happening here. That the scene is full of sexuality is, of course, admitted, but it is not in that way that it shows itself. What Phèdre is doing is allowing herself the luxury of talking to Hippolyte in ambiguous terms. Supposing he were to understand and reply in equally ambiguous terms. What a wonderful conversation there could be! To talk of forbidden things without actually having to mention them, to carry on a conversation which seems to be saying something on one level but is really saying something else on another which could not be put into words would be charming for Phèdre and, to a certain extent, that is what is happening here. She has not yet committed herself. There is still sufficient ambiguity in what she has been saying for her to be able, as she does, to withdraw from a final, irrevocable step. When Hippolyte starts in horror and says:

Dieux! qu'est-ce que j'entends? Madame, oubliez-vous
Que Thésée est mon père, et qu'il est votre époux?
(663-64)

Phédre immediately recoils and assumes an air of injured innocence:

> Et sur quoi jugez-vous que j'en perds la mémoire,
> Prince? Aurais-je perdu tout le soin de ma gloire?
> (665-66)

This is interesting. Racine paints Phèdre as not being at the point
of final defeat yet. She is conscious of her *gloire*, conscious of
her reputation, conscious of her situation, of her status. She is
on the brink of the precipice but she has not fallen over. What
then makes her fall? The fact that Hippolyte makes to leave.
Covered with confusion by the implication given to his stepmother's words, blushing and stammering, his sole wish is to get
out, to remove himself from the sight of the woman whom, so
he thinks, he has so grotesquely insulted. He had imagined that
Phèdre was making love to him! How can he bear to remain with
her after that? So he sets off to go. This is what Phèdre cannot
bear. It had been so sweet letting her imagination range over
delicious possibilities, to see herself and Hippolyte together and
to talk about this dream to him, there in front of her.
Hippolyte's physical presence is so powerful a stimulus for
Phèdre that his sudden removal, the shattering of the dreams,
the end of the self-indulgence is too much. Anything rather than
see Hippolyte go, and so the final, irrevocable step is taken and
Phèdre goes over the precipice. This is how Racine gets his
heroine across this obstacle and pushes her further down the
slope which is leading to destruction. She launches into her
declaration of love which she throws at Hippolyte like a
challenge. The speech is a mixture of love, guilt, shame, self-
abhorrence, yet through it all runs an almost unconscious expression of desire, a desire to force herself on Hippolyte, to
become part of his world:

> Il suffit de tes yeux pour t'en persuader,
> Si tes yeux un moment pouvaient me regarder. (691-92)

The speech works up to a climax in which Phèdre seems to be of-

fering herself to Hippolyte. Here is the sexuality of the scene if it
is anywhere. Phèdre is asking Hippolyte to kill her, but to be
killed by Hippolyte would be almost as ecstatic as to be made
love to by him:

> Voilà mon cœur: c'est là que ta main doit frapper.
> Impatient déjà d'expier son offense,
> Au-devant de ton bras je le sens qui s'avance.
> Frappe.   (704-7)

Here the imperative, the sharp, single syllable of the second
person singular which Phèdre has used throughout this speech
and which always marks in Racine a movement from one emo-
tional plane to another, the moment when restraints are thrown
off and the normal standards of behaviour are no longer the
order of the day, is terrifyingly effective. How much more
powerful is *frappe* than *frappez* would be, and how much more
powerful is the final *donne* with its sonorous echoes which a
great actress will know how to exploit. This is the point in the
play where Racine leaves in no doubt the nature of Phèdre's passion. The violence, the unrestrained voluptuousness with which
she tenders herself to Hippolyte, reveals sexual desire in its most
acute and frenzied state. The verse here is action, and the action
is carried on before our eyes and yet *bienséance* has been strictly
observed. There could be no better example of the way the rules
can be used to create a form of drama which would not exist had
they not existed.

At the end of Act II further news comes from outside. While
passion is raging unrestrained at Trézène moves are being made
elsewhere to deal with the state of affairs that has arisen because
of the 'death' of Thésée. Hippolyte's plan to make Aricie queen
of Athens is, it appears, not going to work as Athens has
declared itself for Phèdre and her son is to have the throne.
Hippolyte's reaction to this piece of news is the marvellously
ironical:

> Dieux, qui la connaissez,
> Est-ce donc sa vertu que vous récompensez? (726-27)

The irony is twofold. On the one hand Hippolyte, unaware at
this moment of how he himself will be affected later on, for the
first time glimpses that in the affairs of this world there is not
necessarily any relationship between what is deserved and what
is awarded. By involving the gods in this he draws attention,
albeit without realising the fact, to the doubtful role of the gods
in dispensing justice. The other irony is, of course, that the
honours that are about to be heaped on Phèdre are useless to
her. The reward that would be most desirable to Phèdre is not
the throne of Athens but the heart of Hippolyte which is forever
denied to her.

Phèdre's role in the third act must be thought of primarily as
showing her responsibility for the accusation that is made
against Hippolyte. This is a crux in the play, as the essence of
Phèdre is that she is morally responsible but is driven to act immorally. Her moral self is constantly there judging and
condemning her other self, and it is the clarity of this vision
which marks her out from other Racinian heroines. How is this
to be reconciled, however, with the action to which she now consents? How far is Phèdre blameworthy in this matter? Racine
gives some clues in his treatment of the moment when this happens which may help in coming to a decision. Phèdre, in Act III,
has renounced her moral self for the time being:

> De l'austère pudeur les bornes sont passées:
> J'ai déclaré ma honte aux yeux de mon vainqueur,
> Et l'espoir malgré moi s'est glissé dans mon cœur.
>
> (766-68)

Deceitful, malignant hope causes more ravages than her passion
had in her moral fibre. Having given expression to her love,
Phèdre now feels justified in what she is doing. Evil-doing
creates its own laws which seem to take precedence over others.
In this scene it is Œnone who is arguing for virtue against
Phèdre's passion. The contrast is brought out strongly in this
scene between Phèdre as she now stands before the world —
responsible for ruling Athens — and Phèdre as she actually is:

> Moi, régner! Moi, ranger un Etat sous ma loi,
> Quand ma faible raison ne règne plus sur moi! (759-60)

Here the use of the political background is exploited to the full. It is at the very moment when Phèdre's moral defences are almost completely breached that her need for them is most imperative in order that she can assume the role that the world is now calling upon her to play. Her vulnerability is now revealed. She seizes on this power that seems to be hers as a means to further her own ends. All pretence, all scruples, all moral considerations are thrown to the winds:

> Sers ma fureur, Œnone, et non point ma raison. (792)

The crown of Athens is to be used as a bait for Hippolyte:

> Va trouver de ma part ce jeune ambitieux,
> Œnone; fais briller la couronne à ses yeux:
> Qu'il mette sur son front le sacré diadème;
> Je ne veux que l'honneur de l'attacher moi-même.
> (799-802)

Thus are grave affairs of state turned into weapons which the passionate use for their own purposes. It is hardly necessary to point out that this is typical of Racine and that Phèdre here is only acting as Pyrrhus or Roxane had acted before her. What is different in the case of Phèdre is that she is acting like this on this one occasion only and is herself aware of the extent to which she is failing to be true to her own moral standards. That is what emerges from the monologue which follows when Œnone departs to try and put her commands into operation:

> Ô toi, qui vois la honte où je suis descendue,
> Implacable Vénus, suis-je assez confondue! (813-14)

Impervious at this moment to moral arguments, how will she react when it is suggested to her that she act immorally? It is precisely when she has allowed this malevolent hope to take possession of her that the news is brought that Thésée is not dead, as had been reported, but alive and present. In order to show Phèdre's reaction Racine has once again recourse to the technique of having Phèdre use her imagination to conjure up a picture. This is how she pictures in her mind's eye the meeting of Thésée, Hippolyte and herself:

> Juste ciel! qu'ai-je fait aujourd'hui!
> Mon époux va paraître, et son fils avec lui!
> Je verrai le témoin de ma flamme adultère
> Observer de quel front j'ose aborder son père,
> Le cœur gros de soupirs qu'il n'a point écoutés,
> L'œil humide de pleurs par l'ingrat rebutés! (839-44)

This is an astonishing passage. There is an interplay of looks and glances which must be analysed to be fully appreciated. Phèdre in her mind's eye sees Hippolyte, 'témoin de ma flamme adultère' (and a witness is someone who has *seen*) looking at her to see how she greets Thésée. She knows that he knows the truth; and he knows that she knows that he knows the truth. Phèdre will be called upon to act a part in front of an audience who knows that a part is being acted. Added to all this is the knowledge of rejection. Her heart is full of sighs 'qu'il n'a point écoutés'; her eyes weep tears 'par l'ingrat rebutés'. We note the use of the word *ingrat*. Phèdre uses the language of the love affair as though she had the right to do so, as though she and Hippolyte were on a par. Such is not the case, and Phèdre will discover this when she learns of the love of Hippolyte and Aricie.

There is still another stage of self-knowledge to be reached. Here, however, we are concerned with the way in which she is brought to give her consent to Œnone's suggestion that Hippolyte should be accused before he has time to reveal what has happened. If we bear the passage just quoted in mind, then the famous line of Phèdre at the approach of Thésée and Hippolyte:

> je vois Hippolyte:

Dans ses yeux insolents, je vois ma perte écrite. (909-10)

takes on its full significance.[12] Phèdre is mistaken. Hippolyte
has no intention of betraying her so there is no need for her to
defend herself against an accusation that never would have been
made. Her imagination is too strong. The vision of what she
thinks would be the case, linked with the look in Hippolyte's
eye, a look interpreted by Phèdre in the light of her own reading
of the situation, is too much for her. She cannot play the part
she knows she ought to play and therefore consents to, or rather
does not dissent from, Œnone's monstrous proposition.
Ironically it is Phèdre's virtue, which will not allow her to act
hypocritically, that is partly responsible for her agreeing to be a
party to a much greater crime, the lie told about Hippolyte. She
cannot, however, escape responsibility for it, nor does she wish
that she should. Her subsequent behaviour shows that. Another
hurdle, however, has been crossed and Racine has created the
dramatic scene to show how that was possible.

Phèdre has not yet reached the end of the road of suffering.
There remains a final step to be taken which will bring her into
depths from whence there is no return, unlike Thésée's from the
'lieux profonds et voisins de l'empire des ombres' (966). *Phèdre*
can be read as a journey of a soul into utter despair. As the
journey progresses the traveller becomes more and more aware
of the nature of it and the ultimate horror of the destination.
Phèdre reaches her destination in the jealousy scene in Act IV. It
was a daring thing for Racine to do because the task he was setting himself seems almost too great. What means can be used to
express further the tortures of his heroine? The means that he
does use illustrate intensely the core of Racinian tragedy. Phèdre
learns of the love of Hippolyte and Aricie from Thésée. Her first
reaction on hearing this is to express the suffering she feels as a
rejected lover. She sees herself in the role of aspirant to the hand
of Hippolyte and scorned by him. Phèdre is deceiving herself
doubly. She is thinking of herself as though she were on equal

---

[12] Jean Pommier (*40*) pp.195-96 drew attention to this episode and commented:
'le noeud de cette tragédie classique, c'est un *malentendu sur un regard*. N'est-ce
pas curieux?' It is going too far to suggest that this is the 'noeud' of the tragedy.

terms with Hippolyte and Aricie, which is not the case, and she is forgetting the nature of her relationship with Hippolyte. On this level she suffers the pangs of jealousy, but she is still able to think of herself as though she could have been loved:

> Peut-être a-t-il un cœur facile à s'attendrir:
> Je suis le seul objet qu'il ne saurait souffrir. (1211-12)

The depth of self-deception on the part of Phèdre is seen here in the use of the phrase 'le seul objet', thereby giving herself a prime place in the consciousness of Hippolyte. Similarly the arrival of Œnone provokes the cry:

> Œnone, qui l'eût cru? j'avais une rivale! (1218)

Phèdre is in no position to have a rival. There was never any question of her being considered a candidate for Hippolyte's love. Yet, at this stage, her suffering develops along these lines and once again her imagination is used to increase her own wretchedness. She conjures up in her mind a picture of the bliss of Hippolyte and Aricie which is contrasted with her own misery. Racine uses the swift, short sentences, the sharp questions to portray the mind in distress. The words reflect the feeling of being caught in a trap from which there is no escape as the mind runs round on itself in a frenzy:

> Comment se sont-ils vus? depuis quand? dans quels lieux?
> Tu le savais: pourquoi me laissais-tu séduire? (1232-33)

Questions are always used by Racine as a means of suggesting a mind that is losing control of itself. Once more Phèdre's imagination takes over and she pictures the young lovers enjoying their love in peace and tranquillity (of course they never have) contrasted with her own unhappiness. Œnone's remark 'Ils ne se verront plus' brings the next stage in Phèdre's descent into horror:

> Ils s'aimeront toujours!
> Au moment que je parle, ah! mortelle pensée!

> Ils bravent la fureur d'une amante insensée!
> Malgré ce même exil qui va les écarter,
> Ils font mille serments de ne se point quitter. (1252-56)

As Phèdre puts into words what she imagines is happening elsewhere, these events assume a terrible reality for her. *Au moment que je parle*, now, this very minute, the immediacy of it is what is so striking and so unbearable. While she, Phèdre, is suffering the tortures of the damned, Hippolyte and Aricie are swearing eternal love for each other. This so-called reality, created by Phèdre out of her own imaginings, pushes her to think of vengeance. Aricie must be punished and Thésée, Phèdre's husband, will be the agent to whom she will turn to avenge her. She sets off to put this plan into operation:

> Dans mes jaloux transports je le veux implorer. (1263)

This is the end of the illusion. At this point reality breaks in to bring Phèdre to an awareness of what she is contemplating doing. The speech changes tone here, and what is remarkable is the way speech and action become one.[13] This is the ultimate justification of the classical form of drama. No other dramatic form could have produced this situation where the words that are spoken constitute the action. Phèdre, when she is speaking now, is not trying to communicate. What she is doing is creating, out of words, her own hell and this hell is herself:

> Que fais-je? Où ma raison se va-t-elle égarer?
> Moi jalouse! Et Thésée est celui que j'implore!
> Mon époux est vivant, et moi je brûle encore!
> Pour qui? Quel est le cœur où prétendent mes vœux?
> Chaque mot sur mon front fait dresser mes cheveux.
>
> (1264-68)

The need to put into words, to say what is, is in itself the drama. This is the clarity of vision with which Racine endows his characters to enhance their sufferings. These questions which

---

[13] For a full discussion of the role of language and speech in Racinian tragedy see Hawcroft (*48*) and Phillips (*53*).

Phèdre asks have horrible answers, and she is not spared this realisation:

> Chaque mot sur mon front fait dresser mes cheveux.
> (1268)

Words become deeds and the deeds are horrible. Thus forced to look at herself Phèdre realises the horror of being what she is: 'Misérable! et je vis!' This is the hell to which she has been brought, and from which there is no escape. For surely this is the meaning of the following lines. Phèdre wants to escape. From what? From herself. Everywhere she turns she sees images of herself. If she looks to the sky, to heaven, what does she find?

> Le ciel, tout l'univers est plein de mes aïeux. (1276)

If she looks to hell, what does she see there? The face of her father, her begetter, surges up in front of her blocking that way. Ultimately there is no escape from oneself, and this is the discovery that emerges. The various steps which have brought Phèdre to this moment of utter despair have been carefully mapped, and the goal of the journey has now been reached. The lucid eye which the heroine turns on the landscape of her suffering is the characteristic which marks the last stage in the tragedy of Phèdre. The cry of *Pardonne* is a cry of despair, an appeal which will not be heard, a symbol of the unfairness of things. Humanity pleads for understanding, which is refused.

The lines which end the speech:

> Hélas! du crime affreux dont la honte me suit,
> Jamais mon triste cœur n'a recueilli le fruit:
> Jusqu'au dernier soupir de malheurs poursuivie
> Je rends dans les tourments une pénible vie. (1291-94)

seem to me to have been much misinterpreted. It is to destroy the whole carefully constructed fabric of this scene to read into these lines a not-very-praiseworthy regret implying that Phèdre would not be suffering what she is now suffering had she been able to enjoy the fruits of the crime with which she reproaches herself. Such an interpretation is unworthy. These lines should be read in conjunction with what precedes to mean that Phèdre, hopelessly and despairingly, offers some small piece of evidence on her own behalf which might mitigate the enormity of the crime that has been committed. In the blackness which she sees when she looks into herself, here is one speck of light, one small compensating factor which might be taken into account. She is not simply regretting that she has never enjoyed what she so much wanted; such regrets would not be in keeping with the tone of the passage. Yet there is more. At this supreme moment Œnone is ready with her excuses. Jean Pommier thinks that it was a mistake on the part of Racine to put in here a passage from Euripides which he had not used earlier and now brings in. [14] This is to miss the point. What Œnone is doing is offering the path of compromise:

> Regardez d'un autre œil une excusable erreur.
> Vous aimez. On ne peut vaincre sa destinée:
> Par un charme fatal vous fûtes entraînée. (1296-98)

These are the excuses by which the weak, mean-spirited human being comes to terms with his own gross imperfections. Without following Lucien Goldmann in all his interpretations of Racine, it is perhaps useful to think of some of his terms when considering this episode of *Phèdre*. Œnone represents the compromise with the world which Phèdre rejects. Phèdre represents the refusal to accept the world and its demand for compromise. She has been destroyed by the world, but she will not now stoop to use the mealy-mouthed excuses which the Œnones of the world have so ready at their disposal to justify their unworthy existences. The explosion of anger which is Phèdre's response to this way of looking at things is magnificent and one of the high points of the tragedy. Phèdre has just descended into the hell which is complete and utter knowledge of oneself. This hell has been hers because of her humanity, the humanity which has betrayed her, but she now rises above her humanity to reject it

14 Pommier (*40*) p.204.

and, in that way, achieves a greatness that makes her noble in spite of what she has done. Pascal had said that man was greater than the universe which destroyed him because man knew what was happening to him, whereas the universe did not.[15] Similarly Phèdre proves herself greater than the forces which destroy her, and when Œnone flings herself into the sea she symbolises Phèdre rejecting these destructive forces which are an inevitable part of being human.

Phèdre appears in the play one more time. At the end of the fifth act, just after Théramène has finished his account of the death of Hippolyte, Phèdre, having taken poison, comes to tell the truth to Thésée. Thésée would prefer not to be told the truth, but ignorance of a truth which would destroy an illusion is a luxury which is not allowed in Racinian tragedy. Phèdre's account of events is bare, unvarnished as befits the situation. After the scene in Act IV there is a difficulty in presenting Phèdre without a sense of anticlimax. This is what Racine avoids. Phèdre really 'dies' at the end of Act IV, scene vi. It is now the shell, the husk of Phèdre that is being destroyed. Hence the language which recounts without emotion the sequence of events. Any other way of presenting the death of Phèdre would falsify the tragedy.

The last words of Phèdre deserve comment. Much has been written about them and, of course, what has been written centres on the metaphor of light and darkness which, running through the play, seems to find here its final expression:

> Déjà je ne vois plus qu'à travers un nuage
> Et le ciel et l'époux que ma présence outrage:
> Et la mort, à mes yeux dérobant la clarté,
> Rend au jour qu'ils souillaient toute sa pureté.
>
> **(1641-44)**

I would like to extend somewhat the significance of these lines, and link them to what Phèdre had done in Act IV, scene vi. By rejecting Œnone, it was suggested, Phèdre was rejecting the world and its compromises. In these lines she would appear to be rejecting the whole of existence, the whole fact of human exist-

15 Pascal, *Pensée* 347 (Brunschvicg edition).

ence on the earth. Because as long as human beings exist the 'jour' will be 'souillé'. For the light to shine out, strong, pure, unsullied there should be nothing there. What could be purer than a world in which there was no existence? 'Pureté' can be achieved only at this price. Thus when the eyes of Phèdre, those eyes which precisely were capable of seeing and understanding 'pureté' but failed in the effort to attain it, when those eyes close in death, which 'rend au jour qu'ils souillaient toute sa pureté', is not the ultimate, tragic message of *Phèdre* being made: that there is no hope, no meaning, no future for a humanity whose very existence stains the great purity of non-existence?

7. Hippolyte and Thésée

The role of Phèdre is so dominant in the play that bears her name that it is easy for the other roles to be overlooked. This is wrong. The play is not a play concentrated on one person, but a gathering together of a number of people and a number of events which combine to form the framework in which Phèdre's tragedy, which is also the tragedy of Thésée, Hippolyte and Aricie, can be unfolded. It behoves us, therefore, not to neglect either Hippolyte and his tragic death nor Thésée and his tragic deception.

The love affair of Hippolyte and Aricie has already been traced to the point where the declaration had been made. The scene with Phèdre and the return of Thésée alter the face of events for Hippolyte, demanding from him a new course of action. What is it to be? The scene between Hippolyte and Thésée (III.v) does not answer this question. Hippolyte asks for permission to leave Trézène, but makes no mention of Aricie. However in the subsequent scene (III.vi) he announces his intention of doing this. The return of Thésée has restored to Hippolyte's passion its full measure of guilt:

> Moi-même, plein d'un feu que sa haine réprouve,
> Quel il m'a vu jadis, et quel il me retrouve! (993-94)

Nevertheless he determines to try and win his father over and gain his consent to a marriage with Aricie. This is the excuse he makes for coming to see Thésée in Act IV, scene ii. Why decide then and not earlier? The answer is to be found in Racine's dramatic method. The springs of the action are used when they are needed, not before, and it is always profitable to look a little closer at the reasons for disposing material in the way in which it is disposed. The scene between Hippolyte and Thésée, while serving the purpose of showing the latter's reaction to his welcome home, is mainly used for 'scenery' purposes. The world outside is being described. Hippolyte wants to go out into the world and prove himself:

> Souffrez que mon courage ose enfin s'occuper:
> Souffrez, si quelque monstre a pu vous échapper,
> Que j'apporte à vos pieds sa dépouille honorable,
> Ou que d'un beau trépas la mémoire durable,
> Eternisant des jours si noblement finis,
> Prouve à tout l'univers que j'étais votre fils. (947-52)

Thus it is that we are reminded of the world outside, the space from which the protagonists come.

Thésée's contribution is of the same order. His account of where he has been reveals too a world of monsters and cruelty. Accompanying his friend Pirithous on a not very respectable expedition, the aim of which was to kidnap the wife of the 'tyran de l'Epire', Thésée finds himself forced to watch his friend being fed to 'des monstres cruels' who lived by eating human beings. The 'tyran' himself will serve as their food when Thésée escapes from his clutches. This is the outside world described by Thésée, anticipated by Hippolyte. Having escaped from the world of monsters Thésée has returned to find — what?

> Je n'ai pour tout accueil que des frémissements;
> Tout fuit, tout se refuse à mes embrassements:
> Et moi-même, éprouvant la terreur que j'inspire,
> Je voudrais être encor dans les prisons d'Epire. (975-78)

He finds fear and terror, almost another prison, more monsters. By insisting as he does on an outside world inhabited by monsters, which is preferable to the world of the play, Racine effectively creates the atmosphere which is appropriate to what is happening.

At the beginning of Act IV we come in at the end of the conversation between Œnone and Thésée. The terrible accusation has been made. The details are vague. When Thésée tries to pin the details down, Œnone evades his questions and leaves them

unanswered. The mechanism of the play demands that it should
be so. There is nothing to be gained by insisting on the fundamental *invraisemblance* of an accusation made and accepted
with so little foundation. Hippolyte appears. He has come to
talk about Aricie. Thésée marvels when he sees him:

> Ah! le voici. Grands dieux! à ce noble maintien
> Quel œil ne serait pas trompé comme le mien? (1035-36)

Thésée's eyes, however, do not deceive him; Hippolyte is what
his appearance suggests he is. It is Thésée who disbelieves the
evidence of his eyes. He immediately launches into his speech of
accusation. It is to be expected that a monster-killer like Thésée
should see in Hippolyte a new kind of monster, a monster whom
it would not be glorious to kill. He thus calls upon Neptune to
avenge him. Racine is able to introduce a fearful irony into the
death of Hippolyte. Thésée's prayer to Neptune is, essentially, a
cry for justice. He has, so he believes, been outrageously
wronged, so wronged that justice is owed to him by the forces
which dispense it, that is to say, the gods. Hippolyte, too,
believes in the gods as purveyors of justice. He says to Aricie in
his interview with her in the first scene of Act V:

> Sur l'équité des dieux osons nous confier;
> Ils ont trop d'intérêt à me justifier... (1351-52)

Never was confidence less well placed. The gods answer Thésée's
prayer, but the answer is not justice but injustice. Hence the
irony. The world in which Thésée and Hippolyte live is not a
world in which justice reigns. This is the same world as that of
Phèdre. As there was no justice for her, neither is there justice
for them. So the intervention of the gods into human affairs in
Phèdre only serves to underline the fundamental absurdity and
unfairness of existence.

Before Hippolyte sets out on the journey which will take him
to his death he has one last interview with Aricie. They plan to
elope. Aricie has been much mocked for her reluctance to run
away with Hippolyte without being assured that he will marry

her. How wrong such mocking is! The moral background of *Phèdre* represents an accepted way of organising human affairs. Abolish marriage and the tragedy of Phèdre herself is at once seriously diminished. Marriage is the institution which commits men and women utterly. Therefore, without making a serious breach in the moral structure of his tragedy, Racine could not allow Hippolyte and Aricie to contemplate not marrying. Hippolyte and Aricie are planning a future, a future in which they will defend themselves if necessary by force and where, again ironically, justice will be rendered to them. The scene thus plays its part in the overall tragic structure by postulating a future that will never be realised, that cannot be realised because it depends for its existence on truth and justice and purity, and these are precisely the qualities that do not exist in the world of *Phèdre*. When the world beckons to Hippolyte and he sets out, at last, from Trézène, we remember the words with which the tragedy opened, but Hippolyte's first journey is to be his last, as is soon told.

The account of Hippolyte's death is given in the famous *récit de Théramène*. The need for this *récit* is obvious. Action which takes place off the stage must be recounted on it and to Thésée's anguished cry: 'Théramène, est-ce toi? Qu'as-tu fait de mon fils?' a reply, and a full one, must be given. The bare fact is told at once: 'Hippolyte n'est plus', for it is not the purpose of the *récit* to keep Thésée on tenterhooks waiting to know what has happened. He is told at once, and then listens to the tale of how his son met his death. Why the long elaborate description? There are surely several explanations. The death of Hippolyte is an unnatural occurrence in more than one sense of the word. He goes to his death because he is the victim of a lie. The universe is going to show how unjust it is by killing him. Thus it is appropriate that more than natural means are used to make his death the unnatural fate it is. Racine decides to keep the monster sent by Neptune out of the deep. It would, let it be noted, be difficult for him to do otherwise in view of the fact that the legend of Hippolyte's death was so well known that to invent some different kind of death for him would have been rash. So the death of Hippolyte is extraordinary and as such merits extraordinary

treatment, although Racine does take care to keep the supernatural element to a minimum. There is a fight between
Hippolyte and the monster in which Hippolyte is victorious in
that he wounds it and, possibly, kills it, so the monster is not
protected by some supernatural means from human attack. This
does not save Hippolyte who dies when his horses bolt, terrified
by the monster. Théramène's description is contrived in such a
way that it arouses both terror and pity and this is, in part, its
justification. The terror is aroused by the description, not so
much of the monster, but of the fatal flight of Hippolyte's
horses; the pity, when Hippolyte dies and is sought by Aricie.
Aricie comes in fulfilment of her promise to meet Hippolyte in
order to marry him and what does she find?

> Elle voit (quel objet pour les yeux d'une amante!)
> Hippolyte étendu, sans forme et sans couleur.
> Elle veut quelque temps douter de son malheur;
> Et ne connaissant plus ce héros qu'elle adore,
> Elle voit Hippolyte, et le demande encore. (1578-82)

These beautiful lines illustrate well the overwhelmingly pathetic
effects that can be achieved by what superficially seem such
simple methods. Racine does not attempt to describe the stricken
Hippolyte, but by letting us look at him through the eyes of his
lover, eyes that look but do not recognise, the horror of what
has happened to him strikes home very forcefully. By emphasis-
ing, through the *récit de Théramène*, the monstrosity of
Hippolyte's death, the grotesque unfairness of it, its consequences for those who loved him, Racine presents another side
of the cruel universe in which the tragedy of *Phèdre* is being
played out.

There remains Thésée. From the point of view of the
mechanics of the play his role is necessary, not only for his
return, which changes the situation so drastically, but also as a
spectator of events in the fifth act. Indeed the theme of this act
could be thought to be the disillusionment of Thésée. He begins
to have doubts about what he has done, although it is not made
clear where these doubts come from, but once they are there,

evidence begins to accumulate that they are justified. Aricie's ambiguous answers to his questioning of her in Act V, scene iii, Panope's news that Œnone has committed suicide and Phèdre is in despair, add so much to his uncertainty that he realises that his world is collapsing around him. Security is gone, and terror takes its place. Quickly, desperately he prays to Neptune not to answer his prayer, but Neptune is deaf to a prayer such as that. Hippolyte is already dead. Just at the moment when he, Thésée, wants to be told that Hippolyte has not been harmed, Théramène arrives with the news that Hippolyte is dead. This is how action is brought onto the stage. This is the perfection of technique for which Racine is so rightly admired. Thésée's role during the scene in which Théramène recounts the death of Hippolyte is to listen. Nobody, not even Phèdre herself, could fulfil this role so effectively. Thésée has sent his son to his death, and must hear how it came about. Not only has he sent a son to his death but what a son, what a magnificent son, what a source of pride and joy!

There is worse to come, for Thésée does not yet know that Hippolyte was innocent of the crime with which he had been charged, and for which he has been punished. This horror is still reserved for him, and he would avoid it if he could:

Je consens que mes yeux soient toujours abusés (1599)

Futile wish! Thésée talks as if he had some control over what happens. It is not for him to consent to anything now. Events have gone far beyond his control. He realises this, in a way, by rejecting the world. Thésée is the third and last of the three to want to flee:

Confus, persécuté d'un mortel souvenir,
De l'univers entier je voudrais me bannir. (1607-8)

This universe in which gods deliver 'faveurs meurtrières' is, like Phèdre's universe, cruel and impassive to human aspirations. Justice, pity, humanity, love are banished from the world which Thésée now inhabits, and his last protection, ignorance of the truth, is about to be torn from him. We have already considered the scene where this is done from the point of view of Phèdre. It is no less significant for Thésée. Thésée is blinded throughout the tragedy, and at the end his blindness is dissipated but in such a way that it would have been better for him to remain blind. The simple world of Thésée, before he found himself in the grip of an incomprehensible situation, was that of monster-killing. He had been a hero in the Herculean mould, but his heroism was of no avail when he was faced with the fact that he was responsible for killing his own son. Thus Racine uses the legend of Thésée, the hero, the killer of monsters, the restorer of peace and tranquillity to places ravaged by brigands, to complete the tragic world of *Phèdre*. In this world heroism is of no account. It exercises itself in vain against the kind of forces that are arrayed against it. Yet it would not be right to say that evil reigns supreme in *Phèdre*. What ultimately emerges is the triumph of nothingness in a universe without a meaning.

Phèdre is, possibly, the greatest of Racine's tragedies. All the elements which combine to form it are already present in his other tragedies. The technique which had obliged him to choose, to prune, to concentrate, had directed his attention to the essence in a set of human relationships. Love, hatred and jealousy were the common stock of seventeenth-century French tragedy, and Racine had already explored fully the means by which these passions could be used to express a tragic interpretation of existence. Each tragedy had brought its own special focus on the problem, and by contrasting notions of innocence and guilt, power and weakness, morality and immorality, Racine had shown how these could be used to show humanity its own face. *Phèdre* mixed the elements in a new way. By combining in one individual the moral sense of an Andromaque and the luxuriant passion of a Roxane, Racine created a character who went to destruction with a terrifying awareness of the process by which this was being brought about. This new way of bringing a searchlight to bear on the sources of action and passion produced new ways of expressing tragic meaning. This is what sets *Phèdre* apart and makes it such a great, such an original work of art. When added to the incomparable use of the dramatic form is found the magical poetry that is Racine's, it is no wonder that the result has fascinated audiences and readers for three centuries.

Bibliography

EDITIONS

There are numerous editions of *Phèdre*, and of Racine's complete works. The following is a selection.

1. *Phèdre*, edited by Philippe Drouillard and Denis A. Canal (Paris: Larousse, 1997). Easily available edition with some useful information.
2. *Phèdre*, edited by Jean Balcou (Paris: Hachette, 1976). In the Nouveaux Classiques Illustrés Hachette series. Contains extracts from Euripides and Seneca and some useful information.
3. *Phèdre*, edited by H.R. Roach (London: Harrap, 1950).
4. *Phèdre*, edited and translated by R.C. Knight (Edinburgh University Press, 1971). An introduction and translation by one of the foremost English Racine scholars.
5. *Phèdre*, mise en scène et commentaires de Jean-Louis Barrault (Paris: Seuil, 1946). An edition in which the great French producer and actor describes his production of *Phèdre*.
6. *Oeuvres*, edited by Paul Mesnard, Les Grands Ecrivains de la France, 8 vols and 2 albums (Paris: Hachette, 1865-73). Still indispensable.
7. *Oeuvres complètes*, edited by Raymond Picard, Bibliothèque de la Pléiade (Paris: Gallimard, 1950). The best complete edition of Racine in manageable form.
8. *Théâtre complet*, edited by J. Morel and A. Viala (Paris: Garnier, 1980). An excellent complete edition of the plays with an interesting dossier on 'Racine aujourd'hui'.

BACKGROUND

9. A. Adam, *Histoire de la littérature française au XVIIe siècle*, 5 vols (Paris: Domat, 1948-56).
10. P. Bénichou, *Morales du grand siècle* (Paris: Gallimard, 1948).
11. R. Bray, *La Formation de la doctrine classique en France* (Paris: Hachette, 1927; Nizet, 1957).
12. G. Brereton, *French Tragic Drama in the 16th and 17th centuries* (London: Methuen, 1973).
13. P. Clarac, *Littérature française*, II, *L'Age classique* (Paris: Arthaud, 1969).
14. G. Lanson, *Esquisse d'une histoire de la tragédie française* (Paris: Champion, 1927).

15. J. Morel, *La Tragédie* (Paris: Armand Colin, 1964).

16. J. Truchet, *La Tragédie classique en France* (Paris: P.U.F., 1975).

17. P.J. Yarrow, *A Literary History of France*, Vol. II, *The Seventeenth Century* (London: Benn, 1967).

RACINE

The bibliography of Racine is so vast that any selection made from it is bound to be imperfect. The following represents old and new approaches together with work devoted exclusively to *Phèdre*.

18. R. Albanese, Jr., '*Phèdre* devant la nouvelle critique', *Les Lettres Romanes*, 31 (1977), 279-291.

19. H.T. Barnwell, 'Racine as plot-maker: seventeenth-century and Sophoclean techniques' in *The Classical Tradition in French Literature, Essays presented to R.C. Knight*, published by the Editors and distributed for them by Grant and Cutler Ltd (London: 1977).

20. R. Barthes, *Sur Racine* (Paris: Seuil, 1963).

21. A. Bonzon, *La Nouvelle critique et Racine* (Paris: Nizet, 1970).

22. P. France, *Racine's Rhetoric* (Oxford: Clarendon Press, 1965).

23. C. Francis, *Les Métamorphoses de Phèdre* (Québec: Editions du Pélican, 1967).

24. J.D. Hubert, *Essai d'exégèse racinienne* (Paris: Nizet, 1956).

25. L. Goldmann, *Le Dieu caché* (Paris: Gallimard, 1955).

26. R.C. Knight, *Racine et la Grèce* (Paris: Boivin, 1950; Nizet, 1974).

27. ——, *Racine. Modern Judgements* (London: Macmillan, 1969).

28. J.C. Lapp, *Aspects of Racinian Tragedy* (Toronto University Press, 1955).

29. G. Le Bidois, *La Vie dans la tragédie de Racine*, 6e édition (Paris: Gigord, 1929).

30. T. Maulnier, *Racine* (Paris: Gallimard, 1936).

31. ——, *Lecture de Phèdre* (Paris: Gallimard, 1942).

32. C. Mauron, *L'Inconscient dans l'oeuvre et la vie de Racine* (Aix-en-Provence: Publications des Annales de la Faculté des Lettres, 1957).

33. G. May, *Tragédie cornélienne, tragédie racinienne* (Urbana: University of Illinois Press, 1948).

34. P. Moreau, *Racine, l'homme et l'oeuvre* (Paris: Boivin, 1943; Hatier, 1952).

35. O. de Mourgues, *Racine or, The Triumph of Relevance* (Cambridge University Press, 1967).

36. W. Newton, *Le Thème de Phèdre et d'Hippolyte dans la littérature française* (Paris: Droz, 1939).

37. A. Niderst, *Les Tragédies de Racine* (Paris: Nizet, 1975).

38. R. Picard, *La Carrière de Jean Racine* (Paris: Gallimard, 1956).

39. J. Pineau, 'La poétique de Racine: l'emploi des mots "amour" et "aimer" dans *Phèdre*' in *Mélanges de littérature française offerts à René Pintard*, Travaux de linguistique et de littérature publiés par le Centre de

Philologie et de Littératures romanes de l'Université de Strasbourg,
XIII, 2 (Strasbourg: 1975).

40.   J. Pommier, *Aspects de Racine* (Paris: Nizet, 1954).
41.   P. Sellier, 'Le jansénisme des tragédies de Racine: réalités ou
        illusion?', *Cahiers de l'Association Internationale des Etudes
        Françaises*, 31 (1979), 135-148.
42.   L. Spitzer, 'The "Récit de Théramène"' in *Linguistics and Literary
        History* (Princeton University Press, 1938), pp.87-134.
43.   E. Vinaver, *Racine et la poésie tragique* (Paris: Nizet, 1951).

Bibliographical Supplement

CRITICISM

44.   J.-L. Backès, *Racine* (Paris: Seuil, Coll. Ecrivains de Toujours, 1981).
45.   R.L. Barnett (ed.), *Relectures raciniennes* (Paris-Seattle-Tübingen:
        PFSCL, Coll. Biblio 17, 16, 1986).
46.   H.T. Barnwell, *The Tragic Drama of Corneille and Racine* (Oxford:
        Clarendon Press, 1982).
47.   M. Fumaroli, 'Entre Athènes et Cnossos: les dieux païens dans
        Phèdre', *Revue d'histoire littéraire de la France*, 93 (1993), 30-62,
        172-90.
48.   M. Hawcroft, *Word as Action: Racine, rhetoric and theatrical
        language* (Oxford: Clarendon Press, 1992).
49.   C.M. Hill (ed.), *Racine: théâtre et poésie* (Leeds: Francis Cairns,
        1991).
50.   E. James and G. Jondorf, *Racine: Phèdre* (Cambridge University Press,
        1994).
51.   D. Maskell, *Racine: a theatrical reading* (Oxford: Clarendon Press,
        1991).
52.   R. Parish, *Racine: the limits of tragedy* (Paris-Seattle-Tübingen:
        PFSCL, Coll. Biblio 17, 74, 1993).
53.   H. Phillips, *Racine: language and theatre* (University of Durham,
        1994).
54.   J. Rohou, *L'Evolution du tragique racinien* (Paris: SEDES, 1991).
55.   ——, *Jean Racine* (Paris: Fayard, 1992).
56.   A. Viala, *Racine: la stratégie du caméléon* (Paris: Seghers, 1990).

TEXTS

57.   *Phèdre*, edited by Richard Parish (Bristol Classical Press, 1996). An
        excellent new edition.
58.   *Théâtre complet*, edited by Philippe Sellier, 2 vols (Paris: Imprimerie
        Nationale, 1995). The most recent complete edition of the plays.
        Phèdre is in Vol.II.

CRITICAL GUIDES TO FRENCH TEXTS

edited by

Roger Little, Wolfgang van Emden, David Williams